COURSE GOALS

This course provides an essential
Using industry-standard image editing, illustration, web design,
animation, audio, and video software, students create an electronic
portfolio that includes text, graphics, animation, video, and sound.
This class is required for all Digital Media certificates and AA degrees
including audio, video, game design and interactive multimedia.

COURSE INFORMATION

STUDENT LEARNING OUTCOMES

- Identify current trends within the digital media industry and identify
  appropriate career opportunities.

- Create and display an integrated digital media portfolio on a website.

OBJECTIVES

Upon completion of this course students will be able to:

1. Discuss current trends in the digital media industry.

2. Research and determine career opportunities in Digital Media.

3. Identify, create, edit, and display different types of digital file formats in
   text, graphics, animation, video, and audio.

4. Create an online digital multimedia presentation using image editing,
   drawing, animation, audio, video and web authoring programs.

USING THIS BOOK AND ACCOMPANYING VIDEOS

Digital Media is a term that applies to so many things it would be
impossible to learn any aspect in great **depth** in one course. This book
provides a **breadth** of information to help you explore fundamental
concepts, industry-standard software tools, and career options. It also
provides step-by-step instruction for all projects you will complete as
part of your electronic portfolio. Use the book as you work through the
lessons. To have the greatest success you will **always** want to watch the
step-by-step videos provided online and in the electronic version of this
book. Hyperlinks in the printed book will require you to type the web
addresses into a browser connected to the Internet.

By the end of the semester you will have created a body of work you will be proud of.

SOFTWARE

Students will use software applications from Adobe's Creative Cloud. This vast array of presentation software makes it easy for digital media specialists to be enormously productive. In this class we will explore the following Creative Cloud components; Bridge, Photoshop, Illustrator, Audition, Dreamweaver, Flash, and Premiere Pro.

You will need to create a subscription through the **Adobe** Creative Cloud or use the Santa Rosa or Petaluma computer labs.

REQUIRED INSTRUCTIONAL MATERIALS

Students will need:

- Access to digital camera and flash drive or cloud storage
- Earphones or headphones for various classroom activities
- Access to the Internet for all hyperlinks (underlined blue text) and video links.
- A Canvas ID Number and Pin Code to access the test, grades, discussion groups, and assignments.

INSTRUCTOR INFORMATION

Instructor: Jeffrey Diamond
Phone: (707) 527-4990
Web Site: http://www.santarosa.edu/~jdiamond
E-mail: jdiamond@santarosa.edu

LOCATION AND CLASS TIMES

To see current schedule of class times go to https://santarosajc.instructure.com/courses/13702

CONTENTS

CLASS ACTIVITIES AND HOMEWORK ASSIGNMENTS

CLASS ONE: DIGITAL MEDIA BASICS

WHAT IS DIGITAL MEDIA?

While there are a million ways to answer that, I think it fitting that it would start with a video. I provide a link to a British video from 2008. Some of the cultural references may get stale over time but the video accurately captures the loud barrage of images, sounds, words, colors, and energy that characterize this era of digital media.

"Digital Media" is everywhere these days, but how do those of us who work within its folds explain it? Watch the video for some ideas. https://www.youtube.com/watch?v=8-5c8pFrFNs

FILE ORGANIZATION

The need to keep your files organized in the field of digital media, and any field related to computers, is required IF you want to be productive. One can spend precious hours over time looking for files because you have not prioritized methods to keep your files organized into projects, fields of interest, time periods, people, etc. While this is a universal theme, it is imperative in digital media, especially with audio and video projects. Mosts video and audio software use the project files as layout tools and simply link to the assets (video files, audio files, images) that are included in the project. As such they are not embedded into the project, they are simply linked. If you do not know where these assets are in relation to a particular project they will not load and the project will not function as expected. It is important to settle on a standard naming convention for files, folders, and directories. For example I name all of my web pages with an underscore separating words, like *contact_us.html.* I name all my programming files with camel-casing the way a programmer would write code. An example of this is *dragAndDrop.fla* I use Adobe Bridge to help me manage all my assets in a intuitive way.

EXAMINE ADOBE BRIDGE

Adobe Bridge is a digital asset management application that allows you to **organize** all sorts of digital media files including but not limited to images, audio, video, animation, electronic books, and text documents. One of its huge benefits is it allows you to preview these files within its application interface without having to launch other programs. You can view content in several workspaces, apply and view Meta data, assign keywords, filter content by file type, date, and many other parameters, even create Web Photo Galleries on the fly (Note: You need the CS6 add-on for this feature in the current CC build).

HOW WILL IT HELP ME?

Imagine you're a photographer that shoots affairs, weddings, quinceaneras, bar or bat-mitzvahs, Sweet Sixteens, Christmas parties. Over a short time you have unwieldy numbers of images and files to deal with. I never heard ANYBODY say, "Gee, I don't have enough files to look through and keep organized." The is what Bridge is for. You spend some time learning it but save much more in the long run. File organization for dates, times, places, file-types, and batch renames are just a few of the skills that digital professionals need that Bridge provides. Whether it be audio, video, image, document, presentation files, Bridge can show you them in the Preview window. No need to launch the native application. This way you can browse, organize, and make decisions quicker with what you want to prioritize for a presentation.

Right-click and choose Save As to download the files for this demonstration

STORYTELLING

Throughout this semester, we will be examining how telling a story is key with all creative art forms. Whether you are creating a photograph, video, illustration, audio production, animation, or website, there should be a story that drives the viewer to want to engage with your work.

Why are stories important? The word story is derived from the Greek word meaning "knowing, knowledge, and wisdom". Since the dawn of humanity we have told stories to connect to each other, to connect the past to the present and to imagine the future. Stories helps us construct meaning.

What are the key elements in a good story?

Andrew Stanton, the writer and filmmaker behind Toy Story, Wall-E, Finding Nemo, and John Carter gave a Ted Talk where he outline some key elements in storytelling. You can watch his entire TED talk here

Stanton suggest that stories MUST:

- Make you care
- Create a promise that they will lead somewhere. This promise must be fulfilled. Even stories with sequels have some levels of completion.
- Create anticipation mingled with uncertainty- what will happen next, at the conclusion
- Make the audience work to figure out the story. Our nature is to solve problems.
- Understand the characters primary motivation. For example Spider-Man's primary motivation is to exorcise the guilt he feels as a result of allowing the robber to get away after committing a petty crime against someone he didn't care about. Later, that same robber killed his beloved Uncle Ben.

A strong theme is always running through a well-told story. One theme used over and over in a variety of ways is the story of triumph over adversity. Slumdog Millionaire is a fine example of this theme. It is the story of a Mumbai teen who becomes a successful contestant on the

Indian version of "Who Wants to be a Millionaire." This theme usually focuses on an exceptional person in a horrible and hopeless situation.

DIGITAL STORYTELLING

If we define storytelling as sharing a sequence of content (beginning, middle, and end) that engages an audience with meaning and emotion, what is the difference between that and **digital** storytelling? Has storytelling changed since the birth of electronic media?

- Here are a few key differences between traditional and digital storytelling:
- Digital stories often have multiple authors. An example would be a blog or twitter feed where many people contribute to stories that develop quickly, Think of the Arab Spring where thousands of people shared their voices and experiences of the events unfolding around them.
- Digital stories can have multiple endings and sometimes do not have any conclusion at all. Think of playing a video game and, depending on your input and role in the game the outcome can change dramatically.
- Digital stories are often "mixed media" experiences which may include text, images, audio, video, and interactive components.
- Digital stories offer the viewer/reader to provide feedback via website forms, within apps, etc.

STORYTELLING WITH IMAGES

A good photo captures the viewer's interest and elicits an emotional response. A photo should engage a viewer by creating a mood, eliciting emotion, hinting at some story sub-plot like a character talking to someone outside of the photograph frame, and suggesting some kind of message. Keep these things in mind when taking your photo.

Sudipta Shaw has written an excellent article on Storytelling Photography in which he states that a photo should affect the user's experience of an image by creating a mood or emotion and/or by conveying a idea, message, or narration. For example, you can create a mood by choosing a background that complments the main subject. Using a black and white, industrial background would effectively complement the mood of a shadowy figure in a trenchcoat. But it wouldn't work to have the background be a sunny scene with the caption "Wish you were here".

HOW TO TAKE GREAT PHOTOS

Go to any photography website and you will be inundated with ideas on best practices for taking good photographs. There are a few things that all photographers agree are key:

Good lighting is key. It is the single most important make or break aspect of a photograph Without good light even the best composition will look grainy and out of balance.

1. Natural light from the sun is the best option.

2. When shooting inside make sure to open blinds and curtains and move the subject near the window but not silhouetted by it.

3. When using artificial light make sure the subject is fully lit. This often requires two lights for balance. If available, use a reflector for a more even spread of light.

Craft your composition in the viewfinder. That means removing any distracting items, making sure not to crop off any crucial portion of your subject, checking that subject's eyes are open, etc.

Keep your subjects close. Faces convey emotion. If you cannot see the details, you cannot feel the emotion. Walk around your subjects and take photos from different angles; above, below, sidelines.

Landscape photographs should have straight horizon lines.
Most cameras and phones have a grid feature that can help with this.

Take lots of photos. After all there's no development expense so go crazy!

Advantages and limitations of Smartphones. They certainly make it more convenient and spontaneous to take pictures and videos. A surprising amount of news and life-events are recorded with these devices that have become our appendages. But remember to always use the rear-facing camera. It is a much higher resolution than the front-facing camera. Also, smartphones take pretty bad pictures indoors, especially in low light. Use natural light whenever possible and check your phone's settings to adjust to the highest possible resolution and click away.

CLASS ONE HOMEWORK- 4 POINTS

4. Create a subscription through the Creative Cloud (or use the SRJC computer labs)

5. Create a folder for ALL classwork

   a. Insert your Flash drive into the computer USB port or on your laptop computer OR Connect to your cloud storage server (such as Google Drive)

   b. Right-click and choose New Folder

   c. Name the folder Introduction to Digital Media- Your Name

   d. Create two sub-folders by right-clicking and choosing New Folder (2x)

   e. Name the folders Homework and Website. It should look like this.

6. Complete the Getting Started Quiz which covers the contents of the website and asks questions about the variety of career options in the field of Digital Media. *Note: You will need your Canvas ID Number and Pin Code to acess this content.* (**2 points**)

Tell me your story (2 points)

Take a "selfie" from the shoulders up and transfer the image to your computer so you can upload it. NOTE: The image should be a .JPG or .PNG file type. Then visit the Class 1: Getting to Know you Discussion page and follow the instructions. *Note: You will need your Canvas ID Number and Pin Code to acess this content.*

7. Start using Adobe TV's hundreds of hours of free videos by watching Learn Photoshop CC; Sections- Get Started and Learn Essentials

8. OPTIONAL- Set up a student.santarosa.edu email account and register for six months free 2-day shipping with an Amazon student account.

CLASS TWO: IMAGE EDITING AND INTERACTION DESIGN

LEARNING TO USE PHOTOSHOP TO EDIT IMAGES

Adobe Photoshop is the de-facto industry standard raster graphics editing software application. It is so synonymous with image alteration that "to Photoshop" or "that picture has been "Photoshopped" are commonly used terms. Photoshop can edit and compose raster images in multiple layers and supports masks, alpha compositing and several color models including RGB, CMYK, and others. In addition to raster graphics, it has limited abilities to edit or render text, vector graphics (especially through clipping path), 3D graphics and video.

But why take pictures and edit them at all? Hopefully to tell a story. For as long as humans existed they told stories with pictures, long before they used written words or even spoke. That's what makes American Sign Language so amazing; signers tell their stories using a language that assigns images to words, which create stories. Whatever your choice of creative medium, its primary role should be to convey your story, experience, view, etc. While it's fine to take snapshots, see if you can tell a story with any image you make.

As we discussed last lesson, a photo should engage a viewer by creating a mood, eliciting emotion, hinting at some story sub-plot, and suggesting some kind of message. Think of the different feeling you get when looking at a black and white photo versus a color photo, or a silhouette versus a brightly lit portrait.

Photoshop Me Artistically is a website/blog that hosts some great examples of storytelling through Photoshopped Art. They also provide the design community with a marketplace and free design advice.

Examine some great examples of Photoshop Manipulation

GET TO KNOW THE PHOTOSHOP TOOLS, WORKSPACE, LAYERS, AND MASKING

TOOLS

The Toolbar in Photoshop has over different tools and another 40 or so when you click and hold on an icon in the Toolbar. Only way to learn it is to do it:)

Tools Panel Overview

A Selection tools
- Move (V)*
  - Rectangular Marquee (M)
  - Elliptical Marquee (M)
  - Single Column Marquee
  - Single Row Marquee
- Lasso (L)
  - Polygonal Lasso (L)
  - Magnetic Lasso (L)
- Quick Selection (W)
  - Magic Wand (W)

B Crop and Slice tools
- Crop (C)
  - Perspective Crop (C)
  - Slice (C)
  - Slice Select (C)

C Measuring tools
- Eyedropper (I)
  - 3D Material Eyedropper (I)
  - Color Sampler (I)
  - Ruler (I)
  - Note (I)
  - Count (I)

D Retouching tools
- Spot Healing Brush (J)
  - Healing Brush (J)
  - Patch (J)
  - Content Aware
  - Red Eye (J)
- Clone Stamp (S)
  - Pattern Stamp (S)

- Eraser (E)
  - Background Eraser (E)
  - Magic Eraser (E)
- Blur
  - Sharpen
  - Smudge
- Dodge (O)
  - Burn (O)
  - Sponge (O)

E Painting tools
- Brush (B)
  - Pencil (B)
  - Color Replacement (B)
  - Mixer Brush (B)
- History Brush (Y)
  - Art History Brush (Y)
- Gradient (G)
  - Paint Bucket (G)
  - 3D Material Drop

F Drawing and type tools
- Pen (P)
  - Freeform Pen (P)
  - Add Anchor Point
  - Delete Anchor Point
  - Convert Point
- Horizontal Type (T)
  - Vertical Type (T)
  - Horizontal Type Mask (T)
  - Vertical Type Mask (T)

- Path Selection (A)
  - Direct Selection (A)
- Rectangle (U)
  - Rounded Rectangle (U)
  - Ellipse (U)
  - Polygon (U)
  - Line (U)
  - Custom Shape (U)

G Navigation tool
- Hand (H)
  - Rotate View (R)
- Zoom (Z)

■ Indicates default tool   * Keyboard shortcuts appear in parenthesis

WORKSPACE

Photoshop has a variety of workspaces to accommodate efficient production techniques. In addition you can create your own custom workspace and easily reset any workspace to its default appearance.

LAYERS

Photoshop layers are like sheets of stacked acetate. You can see through transparent areas of a layer to the layers below. You move a layer to position the content on the layer, like sliding a sheet of acetate in a stack. You can also change the opacity of a layer to make content partially transparent. You use layers to perform tasks such as compositing multiple images, adding text to an image, or adding vector graphic shapes. You can apply a layer style to add a special effect such as a drop shadow or a glow.

LAYER MASKS

Masking layers is a valuable compositing technique for combining multiple photos into a single image or for making color and tonal corrections. You can add a mask to a layer and use the mask to hide portions of the layer and reveal the layers below. Use black to hide a portion of a layer and white to reveal it. In the picture below, the only portion of the top two layers that are revealed are of my dog, Theo.

WHAT IS INTERACTION DESIGN?

Everything you come into contact with in the world has design elements. Whether you are driving a car, using a cell phone, riding a bike, brushing your teeth, your experience is affected by the design of the object. Ever try to open a screw top water bottle while riding a bicycle? Not a good idea. Bicycle water bottles are soft plastic and have pop-up tops for easy access so you can easily open it squeeze the water into your mouth one-handed. As you go through your day try to evaluate the items you use. Which ones are so easy to use you don't have to think about it? These are designed well. Which ones make you engage in trial and error and cause you to make physical adjustments?

The **Interaction Design Association** (IxDA) explains: "Interaction designers strive to create useful and usable products and services. Following the fundamental tenets of user-centered design, the practice of interaction design is grounded in an understanding of real users—their goals, tasks, experiences, needs, and wants. Approaching design from a user-centered perspective, while endeavoring to balance users' needs with business goals and technological capabilities, interaction designers provide solutions to complex design challenges, and define new and evolving interactive products and services."

Payscale.com indicates that in 2014-15 the average Interaction Designer or UX Designer makes nearly $73,000 annually. Salaries start in the high 40s and top out around 120K. There is a high level of job satisfaction in this field. And you have the opportunity to work in a collaborative and creative environment as well as the physicality and psychology of helping design objects for humans. This skill is not at all limited to digital media. Everything we encounter in our day to day lives is designed. We have adapted to it. The consistency, predictability, learnability, of the objects we use whether on computers or in the more sensory world can help or hinder our experiences. If every day you woke up and the coffee pot on button was in a different location or the commode handle had moved you would be both unproductive and incredibly pissed off.

Learn more about this growing field http://vimeo.com/52861634

INTERACTION DESIGN IS ABOUT PEOPLE FIRST.

- What motivates people?
- How do people think?
- How do people behave?

INTERACTION DESIGN IS A USER-CENTERED PROCESS

- Observe

- Define

- Ideate

- Design
  - » Think through steps
  - » Evaluate the presentation
  - » Validate the purpose

- Prototype

- Iterate

- Research guides our iterations

IDEAS COME FROM MANY SOURCES

- Brainstorm

- Create personas

- Conduct task analyses

- Write scenarios

People can provide much information if we observe what they are doing and ask about what they need and expect through:

- Surveys

- Focus groups

- Interviews

INTERACTION DESIGN CORE PRINCIPLES

The user's experience should be:

- Consistent
  - » Differences can attract unwanted attention

- Perceivable

- » Interactions should be obvious
- » Cues- Visual, Auditory, Tactile
- Learnable
  - » Interactions should be easy to learn and remember, intuitive and simple
- Predictable
  - » Where and what should be obvious
  - » When NOT predictable you have guessing, trial and error, failure to interact
- Feedback
  - » Acknowledges interaction

INTERACTION DESIGN STRUCTURE BEST PRACTICES

- Law of Proximity
  - » Objects belonging together
- Law of Similarity
  - » Similar attributes belong together
- Law of Alignment
  - » Things that are aligned are perceived to be more related than things that are not aligned
  - » Western readers read top down and left to right. Elements that follow this pattern influence perception and behavior
- Follow "Desire Lines"
  - » Allow users to lead designers development of methods of interaction
  - » Observation of use of a product can uncover how people use it. Change the design accordingly.
- Top-Down Lighting Bias
  - » Objects light on the top appear 3D
  - » Objects look most natural when lit from the top-left and look scary when lit from below

EFFECTIVE NAVIGATION

- Present and Available
  - » Consistent
  - » Contextual links vary
- Placing Navigation
  - » Web sites- Horizontal rows or vertical columns

» Mobile sites- Vertical stack at top or bottom, or "rolled up" into a menu or button

- Search and Filtering
  » Search is an expected feature, filtering helps limit information
- Navigation should NOT be a scavenger hunt

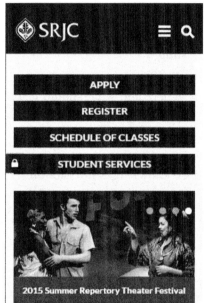

IMAGES

- Object > Stimulus > Perception > Meaning
- Sensory Filtering
  » We ignore most information and pay attention to a small amount- designers must focus users' attention
- Responding to Color
  » Trichromatic Theory- All colors we see are composed of red, green, and blue light
  » Our color sensitivity peaks at YELLOW
- Images and Graphics
  » Faces and illustrations draw attention before blocks of text
- We can use eyesight to direct a user's attention to text

MOTION

- Used to direct attention
- Motion can distract
  » Peripheral changes can pull our eye away from what we want the user to focus on

- Effective Motion
  - » When our INTENT is to cause the user to see the content move from one location to another
- Video Considerations
  - » Avoid auto-play
  - » Provide media controls and status information

SUMMARY

Essential Principles of interaction Design include:

- Consistency

- Perceivability

- Learnability

- Predictability

- Feedback

- These Principles form a system we learn and use to make the user experience successful

Learn what interactive design is from graphic design consultant Chanelle Henry- http://www.howcast.com/videos/509204-What-Is-Interactive-Design-Graphic-Design#

CLASS TWO HOMEWORK- 6 POINTS

1. Review the Principles of Interaction Design (pp.20-23)

2. Complete the Principles of Interaction Design quiz (2 points)

3. Watch and practice Edit your first photo in Photoshop

4. Choose Photoshop Assignment option 1 or 2 on the following pages (4 points).

OPTION 1-CREATE A PANORAMA

1. REQUIRED- Watch this video demonstration (use the PAUSE button to jump between watching the video and completing the steps in Photoshop)

2. Use a digital camera to create **your own images** for the panorama. Make sure to shoot in portrait mode and overlap your pictures by around 10% so Photoshop can stitch them together easily.

3. Open Photoshop and create a multiple image panorama (3 images)

4. Image must use a layer of type, and a shape layer with an accompanying mask that blends the shape into the overall image as demonstrated in the instructor's video.

5. Once you have completed all the steps in the video demonstration above, select Image>Size and make sure Image size is 10 MB or less. If it is bigger reduce the percentage until the updated size is below 10 MB and click OK.

6. Save the image as **class2.psd** into the homework folder of your flash drive. Upload it to the Intro to Digital Media dropbox (using your CATE ID Number and Pin Code). **Leave the background layer, shape layer, and text layers intact.**

7. Navigate to this week's Assignment page (You will need your **Canvas** ID Number and Pin Code).

8. Click on the **Submit Assignment** Button at the top of the Assignment page.

9. Click the **Choose File** button

10. Select your **class2.psd** file and click Open

11. Click the **Submit Assignment** button. (4 points)

OPTION 2- CREATE A MULTIPLE EXPOSURE SHOT

1. REQUIRED- Watch the video demonstration

    a. Right-click and Save as to use these files for practice while attempting the project. You CANNOT use these files for your homework submission..

2. Use a digital camera to create your own images and create a multiple exposure as per the video demonstration

3. In Photoshop choose File> Export> Export As

4. Select Format>JPG from the drop-down menu in the top right corner

5. Reduce the width to 1024 under Image Size

6. Select Export and save as **class2.jpg** into your homework folder

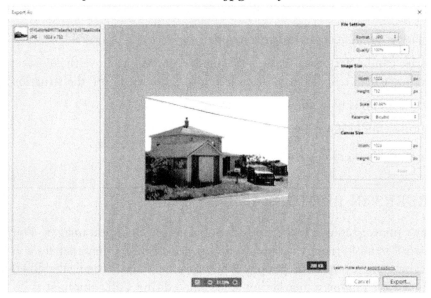

7. Navigate to this week's Assignment page (You will need your **Canvas ID Number** and Pin Code).

8. Click on the **Submit Assignment** Button at the top of the Assignment page.

9. Click the **Choose File** button

10. Select your **class2.jpg** file and click Open

11. Click the **Submit Assignment** button. (4 points)

CLASS THREE: IMAGE EDITING- TONAL AND COLOR ADJUSTMENTS AND ADJUSTMENT LAYERS

MORE STORYTELLING WITH IMAGES

Novelist Tracy Chevalier, the author of "Girl With a Pearl Earring" has a very interesting talk about how finding the story behind painting can help us enjoy them more. We are constantly telling stories, about our friends, future and past selves, strangers. When we examine images more closely, paying attention to facial expressions, body language, colors, image elements, we can have a richer experience. Here is a link to her entire TED talk.

How can you make it easier for the viewer to find the story in your images? David Peterson, a well-known photographer offers these tips:

• Isolate your subjects to create a mood

• Stories can be fictional. Create a dramatic scene and remove the elements that don't help tell the story, even if it alters the reality of the situation.

• Get your subjects to show more emotion.

• Capture candid moments or make it seem you have.

You can read Peterson's entire article here.

CAREERS IN PHOTOGRAPHY

Today's photographers work almost exclusively with digital images. They find work in advertising, fashion, wedding, documentary, newspapers and magazines, and event photography. Photographers need technical skills for configuring equipment, marketing skills, and editing skills amongst others. Editing skills include ability to process and edit digital images in a host of ways which we will examine in our exploration of Adobe Photoshop, the industry-standard tool for photo editing. In 2015, the projected growth in the field of photography as 4 percent, slower than the average of all occupations. This is certainly tied to how digital photography provides the layperson very advanced photography tools.

Watch Careers in Photography with Tom Schierlitz, Photographer https://www.youtube.com/watch?v=3iCaDJoqcNY&list=PL3710778E173F59BD

NONDESTRUCTIVE IMAGE EDITING WITH PHOTOSHOP ADJUSTMENT LAYERS

An adjustment layer applies color and tonal adjustments to your image without permanently changing pixel values. For example, rather than making a Levels or Curves adjustment directly to your image, you can create a Levels or Curves adjustment layer. The color and tonal adjustments are stored in the adjustment layer and apply to all the layers below it. You can discard your changes and restore the original image at any time. There are 15 different types of adjustment layers which adjust everything from color, brightness, saturation, and a variety of filters as part of that set.

Adjustment layers provide the following advantages:

• Nondestructive edits. You can try different settings and re-edit the adjustment layer at any time. You can also reduce the effect of the adjustment by lowering the opacity of the layer.

• Selective editing. Paint on the adjustment layer's image mask to apply an adjustment to part of an image. Later you can control which parts of the image are adjusted by re-editing the layer mask. You can vary the adjustment by painting on the mask with different tones of gray.

• Ability to apply adjustments to multiple images. Copy and paste adjustment layers between images to apply the same color and tonal adjustments.

• Adjustment layers have many of the same characteristics as other layers. You can adjust their opacity and blending mode, and you can group them to apply the adjustment to specific layers. Likewise, you can turn their visibility on and off to apply or preview the effect.

PHOTOSHOP LAYERS & MASKS EXPLORATION

- To explore using layers to tell a story with Photoshop, right-click and Save Link As to download the exercise files

- Watch the Layers video

- OPTIONAL- Upload your version of the Layers demo for two extra-credit points. Name the file week3_ec.PSD. Leave ALL layers intact.

CLASS THREE HOMEWORK- 4 POINTS

Watch the video demonstration of homework for week three- Based on the techniques presented in the video demonstration:

1. Take a photo of someone you admire, preferably in a field of digital media (audio engineer, video producer, game designer, web designer, etc.). Note: This cannot be pictures you find on the Internet. If you use those, it will be very easy for me to find the same images quickly.

2. Import and open the image in Photoshop.

3. Create a Curves Adjustment Layer to correct the tonality of the duplicate layer as per the video demonstration.

4. Select File> File Info, and in the Description field, write a one paragraph explanation of who the person is and why you admire them.

5. Leave the layers intact and save the file as **class3.psd** into the homework folder on your Flash drive or cloud storage drive

6. In Photoshop choose File> Export> Export As

7. Select Format>JPG from the drop-down menu in the top right corner

8. Reduce the width to 1024 under Image Size

9. Select Export and save as **class3.jpg**

10. Navigate to this week's Assignment page (You will need your **Canvas** ID Number and Pin Code).

11. Click on the Submit Button at the top of the Assignment page.

12. Choose your **class3.psd and your class3.jpg** files and click the Submit Assignment button.

CLASS FOUR: ILLUSTRATOR ESSENTIALS

Adobe Illustrator is used for creating vector based illustrations such as logos, branding elements, and designs for both print and web. The advantage of vector graphics is that they can be scaled up or down without losing any resolution or clarity. Illustrator is not the go-to program for creating brochures but is perfect for creating design samples for billboards, t-shirts, business cards, letterheads and fliers; all in one document. It is also useful for digitizing scanned artwork, creating wireframe drawings and making digital paintings. It is also a go to tool for the design and creation of logos. We will be exploring logo design with Illustrator in class five. For this class right-click and Save Link As to download the Illustrator files we will use to explore Illustrator's drawing tools.

EXPLORE ILLUSTRATOR

HOW TO SET UP A NEW DOCUMENT

You can create new Illustrator documents from a new document profile or from a template. Creating a document from a new document profile gives you a blank document with the selected profile's default fill and stroke colors, graphic styles, brushes, symbols, actions, viewing preferences, etc. Creating a document from a template gives you a document with preset design elements and settings.

You create a new document from the Welcome screen, or by choosing File > New. To view the Welcome screen, select Help > Welcome. New documents can contain multiple artboards. This is often useful when you want to have graphic designs for business cards, letterheads, logos, t-shirt designs for an individual product or client all in one file.

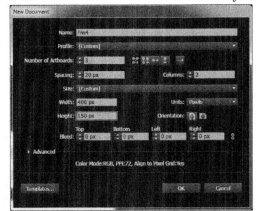

WORK WITH ARTBOARDS

You can use multiple artboards for different outputs such as business cards, billboards, and letterheads all within the same Illustrator file.

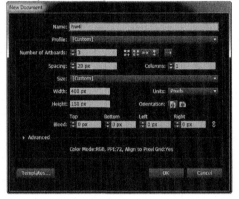

SHAPE TOOLS

Some examples of shape tools include the rectangle, rounded rectangle, ellipse, polygon, and star tool. These tools are used extensively in creating the vector artwork commonly associated with Illustrator. You modify the shapes by accessing the Options bar at the top of the document window. This allows you to edit the stroke, fill, line thickness and many other features that can be applied to your shapes.

OPTIONS BAR

The Options bar allows you to control a variety of properties of the object selected. The appearance of the options within the bar depend upon the object currently selected. In the example below, we see the options associated with a path created with the Ellipse shape tool.

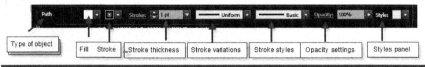

BRUSHES

The easiest way to use brushes is to select the Paintbrush tool from the toolbar. The options bar allows you to edit the setting of any brush. For example, you can open an existing piece of artwork, select a path within that artwork and apply a brush to the selected path either by clicking on a brush style in the Options bar or by selecting a brush from the brushes panel. In addition, the Brushes panel provides access to an entire selection of Libraries that give you access to hundreds of custom brushes.

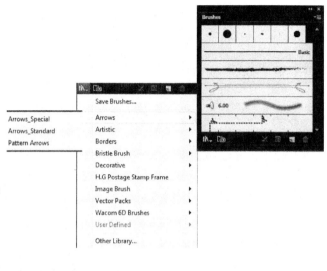

APPLYING COLORS

When creating and editing objects in Illustrator you access color information in several places. For example, if you create a rectangle and select the object, you will see both stroke and fill color information both at the bottom of the Toolbar and in the Option bar at the top of the document window. To change color of the stroke you first make sure the stroke is in front of the fill color at the bottom of the toolbar, then roll your cursor over the Color panel. The cursor becomes an eyedropper. Now click on the color you want to use. You can also change the color by rolling the cursor over the Swatches in the panel below the Color panel. In addition, you can access the swatches from the Options bar. Finally, you can double click on the color directly in the toolbar. This will bring up the color spectrum ramp where you can pick your color. You can also pick NONE

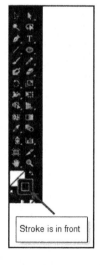

Stroke is in front

for the color of either stroke or fill from all the locations discussed above.

You would use this same approach with changing the fill color but first

would need to click on the fill color chip and select Swap Fill and Stroke to move it to the front.

WORKING WITH TYPE

Adobe Illustrator excels at providing artists with control over the appearance of their type within a document. With the Type tool selected you can either, click and drag within a document to create a text box within which you can type (Area Type) or you can simply click and type (Point Type). In this case the type would continue until you entered a line break. In addition, you can

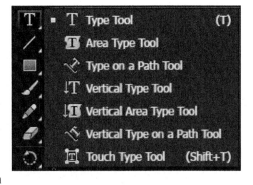

Type on a Path by clicking and holding down the mouse while selecting the Type Tool. You will see the Type on a Path icon. When you select this tool and click on a simple path your text will follow the path.

You can control the appearance of your type from both the Options bar and the Type panels.

The Character panel allows you to change fonts, control the font size, kerning, leading, tracking, height, width, rotation, and more.

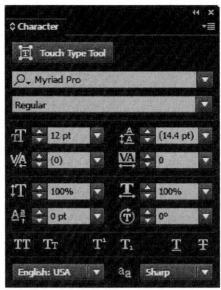

The Paragraph type panel allow you to modify the paragraph alignment, indentation, and spacing.

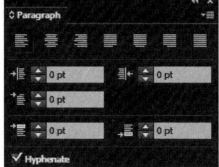

TRANSFORMING ARTWORK

The Free Transform tool allows you to rotate, resize, skew, constrain, free distort, and perspective distort. Note: You must make sure to activate the object you want to transform by using the Selection tool before using the Free Transform tool.

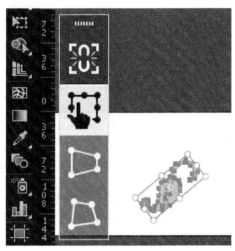

HOW TO SAVE A FILE FOR OUTPUT

You can select File> Save to save a native Illustrator file. You can also save the file as PDF or EPS files. These are often preferred by print shops. For websites or other image editing work you have the ability to save your Illustrator document as PNG, JPG, GIF, and PSD (Photoshop) files. You can either choose File> Save for Web or File> Export. The advantage of choosing export is that it allows you to save multiple artboards as individual files.

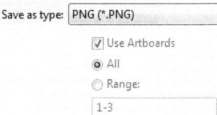

TOOL PANEL OVERVIEW

SELECTION TOOL GALLERY

- The Selection tool (V) selects entire objects.
- The Direct Selection tool (A) selects points or path segments within objects.
- The Artboard tool creates separate artboards for printing or export.

DRAWING TOOL GALLERY

- The Pen tool (P) draws straight and curved lines to create objects.
- The Add Anchor Point tool (+) adds anchor points to paths.
- The Delete Anchor Point tool (-) deletes anchor points from paths.
- The Convert Anchor Point tool (Shift + C) changes smooth points to corner points and vice-versa.
- The Line Segment tool (\) draws individual straight line segments.
- The Rectangle tool (M) draws squares and rectangles.
- The Ellipse tool (L) draws circles and ovals.
- The Polygon tool draws regular, multi-sided shapes.
- The Star tool draws stars.
- The Pencil tool (N) draws and edits freehand lines.
- The Perspective Grid allows creating and rendering artwork in perspective.

TYPE TOOL GALLERY

- The Type tool (T) creates individual type and type containers and lets you enter and edit type.
- The Area Type tool changes closed paths to type containers and lets you enter type within them.
- The Type On A Path tool changes paths to type paths, and lets you enter and edit type on them.

PAINTING TOOL GALLERY

- The Paintbrush tool (B) draws freehand and calligraphic lines, as well as art, patterns, and bristle brush strokes on paths.

- The Live Paint Bucket tool (K) paints faces and edges of Live Paint groups with the current paint attributes.

RESHAPING TOOL GALLERY

- The Rotate tool (R) rotates objects around a fixed point.

- The Reflect tool (O) flips objects over a fixed axis.

MOVING AND ZOOMING TOOL GALLERY

- Illustrator provides the following tools for moving around in and controlling the view of the artboard:

- The Hand tool (H) moves the Illustrator artboard within the illustration window.

- The Zoom tool (Z) increases and decreases the view magnification in the illustration window.

ADOBE ILLUSTRATOR CC
Cheat Sheet

TOOLS PANEL OVERVIEW

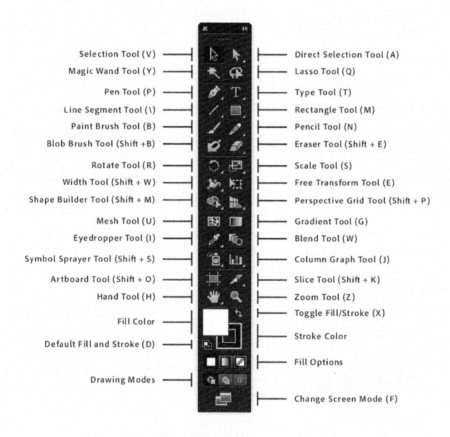

Selection Tool (V) ——— Direct Selection Tool (A)
Magic Wand Tool (Y) ——— Lasso Tool (Q)
Pen Tool (P) ——— Type Tool (T)
Line Segment Tool (\) ——— Rectangle Tool (M)
Paint Brush Tool (B) ——— Pencil Tool (N)
Blob Brush Tool (Shift +B) ——— Eraser Tool (Shift + E)
Rotate Tool (R) ——— Scale Tool (S)
Width Tool (Shift + W) ——— Free Transform Tool (E)
Shape Builder Tool (Shift + M) ——— Perspective Grid Tool (Shift + P)
Mesh Tool (U) ——— Gradient Tool (G)
Eyedropper Tool (I) ——— Blend Tool (W)
Symbol Sprayer Tool (Shift + S) ——— Column Graph Tool (J)
Artboard Tool (Shift + O) ——— Slice Tool (Shift + K)
Hand Tool (H) ——— Zoom Tool (Z)
Fill Color ——— Toggle Fill/Stroke (X)
Default Fill and Stroke (D) ——— Stroke Color
Drawing Modes ——— Fill Options
——— Change Screen Mode (F)

CLASS FOUR HOMEWORK- 2 POINTS

1. Go to the Adobe TV website and watch the Illustrator videos; including all **Essential for Beginners** (8 short videos)

2. Complete the **How to design a logo with Illustrator** project available on the Adobe tutorials page

3. Save as **class4**.AI into the homework folder on your Flash drive or cloud storage drive

4. Navigate to this week's Assignment page (You will need your **Canvas** ID Number and Pin Code).

5. Click on the **Submit Assignment** Button at the top of the Assignment page.

6. Click the **Choose File** button and select your **class4**.AI file then click Open

7. Click the **Submit Assignment** button.

CLASS FIVE: EXPLORING IDENTITY DESIGN

The word **identity** has many meanings from how we define ourselves to how others define and identify with us. In the business world, IDENTITY is the internal image of a business and describes how they want to be perceived by the public. Logos are a fundamental extension of that identity and brand and helps tell the STORY of the brand. A good logo adds definition to a brand and helps visually explain a brand. Many brands rely on subliminal and more direct techniques to tell the story of the brand. See if you can find the story of the brand hidden within these logos.

GRAPHIC DESIGN CAREERS

Graphic Design encompasses a wide variety of occupations including Graphic Art Managers, Creative Director, Production Manager, Brand Developer, Logo Designer, Illustrator, Multimedia Developer, Visual Journalist, Interface Designer, Web Designer, and more. Salaries vary widely. Graphic Designers are the people responsible for the rendering of the client's vision of their brand and identity into a logo. The video below gives you a glimpse into a working graphic artist.

https://www.youtube.com/watch?v=BmBK0_vbYnY

IDENTITY, BRAND, AND LOGO EXPLAINED

Identity- Refers to all the company materials with which they market their brand.

An identity is:

- The different physical elements of the company that customers come in contact with

- The complete package of company materials: logo, business cards, email signatures, websites, ads, employee uniforms, store layout, package design, corporate jingle, etc.

Brand- The word brand originally came from branding cattle, a stamp of ownership. Later it came to represent a guarantee of good quality.

A brand is:

- A concept, not a concrete object

- The foundation of your entire marketing framework

- What people think and feel when they experience your company (their gut feeling)

Logo- Paul Rand, one of the world's greatest designers says that "a logo is a flag, a signature, an escutcheon, a street sign. A logo does not sell (directly), it identifies.

A logo is:

- The emblem or mascot of the organization

- The element that triggers an emotional response and sense of allegiance from consumers
- A trademark

Watch the video on the assignment page for an excellent explanation of logos https://www.youtube.com/watch?v=JKIAOZZritk

---

PRINCIPLES OF EFFECTIVE LOGO DESIGN

There are many principles one can find related to effective logo design. Many experts agree that if you had to choose five essential principles they would include the following explanation and principles:

A good logo is distinctive, appropriate, practical, graphic and simple in form, and it conveys the owner's intended message. You should follow the five principles below to ensure that your design meets all of these criteria:

Simple	Memorable	Timeless	Versatile	Appropriate

CLASS FIVE HOMEWORK- 6 POINTS

1. Review the 5 principles of effective logo design
2. Look at some example identities
3. Think about how your logo is connected to the field you want to work in and/or your personal brand. Make sure there is a strong connection between your imagery and tagline and the product/services/brand you are representing.
4. Review logo creation and typography techniques we explored in class
5. Use Adobe Illustrator to create three different identity designs:
6. Select File> New> and in the New Document dialog box set to the specifications in the image on the following page.

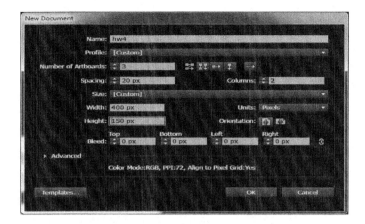

7. Requirements: Use both Adobe Illustrator text and drawing tools that we explored in class to create three different designs.

- Adhere to the 5 principles of effective logo design

- Include a tag line with each logo AND text connected to a path

- Use at least 2 text adjustments (kerning, scaling, leading, rotation) that we explored in class

- Choose fonts appropriate for your message

- Limit colors to three (in addition to black and white). **No gradients.**

- Select File> File Info, place your cursor in the description field and list the 5 principles of effective logo design. Write two or more sentences describing how your logo meets these principles. Include a list of 5 or more words that describes the feelings you want the logo/identity to portray and list of 5 or more words describing the product/brand you are designing for.

8. Save as **class5.AI** into the homework folder on your Flash drive

9. Choose **File> Package** and save the package as class5_folder

10. Right-click and choose Send to Compressed folder (Windows) or Compress Folder (Mac) and save as **class5.zip**

11. Navigate to the Assignment page

12. Click on the **Submit Assignment** Button at the top of the Assignment page.

13. Click the **Choose File** button and select your **class5**.AI file then click Open

14. Click the **Submit Assignment** button.

CLASS SIX: DIGITAL AUDIO FUNDAMENTALS

WHAT IS DIGITAL AUDIO?

Digital audio is either created on a digital device like a computer or tablet OR is the process of converting an analog sound into a form where it can be stored and manipulated digitally.

KEY AUDIO TERMINOLOGY

- Digital Sampling is the process of sampling analog waveforms at evenly spaced time points. Each sample is represented as a precise numeric value. It is then digitally stored for listening, editing, mixing, etc.
- Digital Audio Quality is determined by the sample rate and bit depth of the digital recording.
    - » Sample Rate- The higher the sample rate the more accurate the sound
        - » CD- 44.1 KHz- 44,100 samples of music per second
        - » When you create a new file you can choose the sample rate (44 for audio 48 for video)
    - » Bit Depth is the number of bits (zeros and ones) used to represent each sample
        - » Determines the dynamic range of audio file
        - » The more bits, the wider the range of the sound sample
            - » 8 bits- 48 dB of range
            - » 16 bits- 96 dB of range
            - » 32 bit (float)- best choice
- Frequency
    - » Timing of sound waves hitting your eardrum measured in Hz (cycles per second)
    - » Piano ranges from 32 Hz to 4186 Hz
    - » Human hearing- 20 Hz to 20,000 Hz (20 KHz)
    - » Important in working with Spectral Frequency window
- Amplitude
    - » Loudness or volume of a sound
    - » Frequency and amplitude give you pitch and loudness of sound
    - » Measured in decibels (dB)

AUDIO ENGINEERING CAREERS

Audio engineering is a promising career that offers immense opportunity in film, video production, sound broadcasting and advertising. Audio engineers are employed in many industries and settings including movies where they are used for voice overs, sound tracks, sound effects and more. They play a major role in the music industry as sound board mixers, audio engineers in studios and for live concerts, and many other settings. They are an essential part of the gaming industry where they provide their expertise in the many sounds that bring video games to life. On a more day-to-day basis audio engineers are used in home audio stores, at family and corporate events, for sporting and school events, and in ways that are just emerging now. According to payscale.com, an Audio Engineer earns an average salary of $44,465 per year.

Watch "What does and Audio Engineer do?"
https://www.youtube.com/watch?v=9yRA8K0pY1Y

.INTRODUCING AUDITION

While many audio engineers use Avid Pro Tools as the software of choice, Adobe Audition has become a very powerful tool in its own right, especially in terms on integrating with Premiere Pro to produce professional quality content. Adobe Audition is a 64-bit audio editing application which maximizes the use of system memory or RAM far beyond the 3 Gigabyte limit of the 32-bit application. As with most other applications in the Adobe Creative Cloud, Audition works Mac or PC, exactly the same and the files that you create on one platform are compatible with the other.

Audition has two paradigms within which to work; the Multi-track Session Editor and the Wave Form editor. The multi-track editor allows you to control a large variety of sound elements for a multitude of files. The Waveform Editor allows you to do serious editing on individual sounds files. Audition also has a very intuitive set of playback controls.

Adobe Audition Waveform Editor

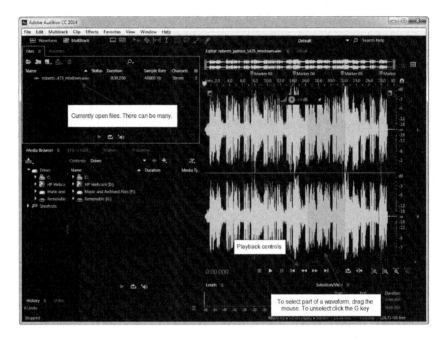

Adobe Audition Multitrack Editor

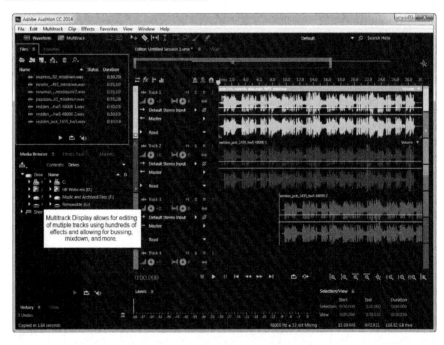

One VERY IMPORTANT thing to remember when creating audio and video projects that is distinctly different from working with Adobe Photoshop or Illustrator is that **you must keep all your support files when working in a project.** In other words, when creating a project with Audition for audio or Premiere for video, the project file simply points to the imported images, sounds, video clips etc. They are not embedded in the project and you need those separate files for the duration of the project.

EXPLORING ADOBE AUDITION

- Waveform vs. Multitrack Mode
  - » Multi- multi controls, combine sounds, mixing
  - » Waveform- individual audio files, spectral frequency display, use brush tool to select portion of sound
- Interface- Waveform vs Multitrack options change contextually
  - » Both modes have playback controls
  - » Lots of preset layouts
  - » Files panel, search box, filter box
  - » Media Browser- check for files and bring into Projects panel
  - » Markers, Properties, History, Video panels
- Preferences
  - » Audio Hardware- changes according to your OS (Windows- ASIO device class is best)
- Audio Channel Mapping- You can set which channels map to input and output

IMPORTING AND MANAGING MEDIA FILES

- Importing is creating shortcut- you need the support files for each project
  - » You can import, open, or open in Media Browser (can view without importing)
- Extracting tracks from a CD
  - » File> Extract from CD
  - » Within Extract dialog box you can set ID3 info (meta data), manually rename tracks, preview tracks
- Creating a new audio file
  - » File> New Audio File, also keyboard shortcut
  - » Can set various parameters in New Audio File dialog box- 48 KHz, Stereo, 32 bit

- Recording an Audio File
  - » Click red button to define specs on new file
  - » Check levels- choose meter input signal, don't go over 0
  - » Control S to save
- Importing video files
  - » Can use video clip as reference for audio recording- good for multitrack
  - » Can edit the audio in waveform view. Working with Sound Files

WORKING WITH SOUND FILES

- Comparing waveforms- vertical axis indicates amplitude
  - » Spectral frequency display- vertical axis indicates frequency, brightness indicates amplitude
- Spectral pitch display- identifies notes- blue line identifies main body of pitch, good for working with pitch bender and pitch correction

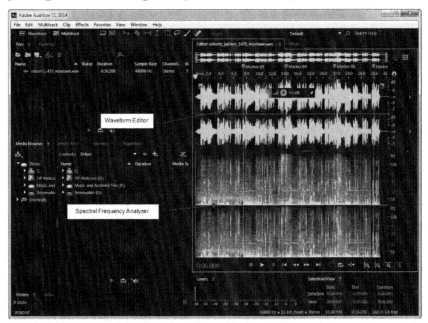

Spectral Pitch Display Window

- Making selections- Double-clicking selects entire audio file.
- Marquee Tool- select specific frequencies inside of the spectral display.
- Lasso tool allows you to be more specific with frequency selection.
- Using playback controls- shows, levels, selection, timecode, markers, and

all standard playback control options. Can use J (backwards), K (pauses), and L (forwards) keys to shuttle controls.

- Using zoom controls- can control time and amplitude measurement scales. Buttons at the bottom allow you to zoom in and out of time or (with Option key) amplitude. Zoom out full allows you to see entire audio file in window.

- Markers- Press M key to add marker. Use Marker panel to rename markers. Set duration in Marker window. Added to Meta data of file. You can export markers from long audio files.

- Paintbrush selection tool- Can set size, pixels, and opacity to audio selection. Spot healing brush tool removes sounds within a selection.

WAVEFORM & SPRECTRAL FREQUENCY ADJUSTMENTS

Download practice files here

- Using the Heads-Up Display to reduce or increase amplitude
- Normalizing audio levels- Choose Window> Match Volume window. Use compute average volume button.
- Adding fades- Square in top corners of waveform display window allows fade ins and outs. You can create infinite curves of fades.
- Noise Reduction Techniques- Noise Reduction and Sound Remover
- Tools- Selection tools for sound removal, and Auto Healing

CLASS SIX HOMEWORK- 2 POINTS

1. Bring your flash drive
2. Watch Learn Audition CC; Noise removal, Audio cleanup, and Audio Effects.
3. Watch Removing Background Distractions
4. Right-click on this file and save to your homework folder
5. Edit the start file and use the tools indicated in the instructional video to remove background noises and enhance the speech.
6. Export the file as **class6**.WAV
7. Navigate to the Assignment page
8. Click on the **Submit Assignment** Button at the top of the Assignment page.
9. Click the **Choose File** button and select your **class6.wav** file then click Open
10. Click the **Submit Assignment** button.

CLASS SEVEN: USING AUDITION TO EDIT AND EXPORT SOUND FILES

MORE FEATURES

- **Effects controls-** Audition has many effects presets and controls that enable you to customize sounds. The Effects Rack lets you insert, edit, and reorder up to 16 effects, optimize mix levels, and store favorite presets. Most rack controls appear in both the Waveform and Multitrack editors.

- **Cleaning up Audio-** Noise reduction and audio cleanup techniques include the use of effects such as the Click/Pop Eliminator, visually fading and changing amplitude, identifying noises visually with the Spectral Frequency Analyzer to edit out unwanted frequencies such as cell phones, and more.

- **Multitrack Editing-** In the Multitrack Editor, you can mix together multiple audio tracks to create layered soundtracks and elaborate musical compositions. You can record and mix unlimited tracks, and each track can contain as many clips as you need—the only limits are hard disk space and processing power. When you're happy with a mix, you can export a mixdown file for use on CD, the web, and more.

- **Sending a sequence from Premiere Pro to Audition-** Adobe Audition lets you edit directly from Premiere Pro. When you right-click on an audio track in Premiere Pro and choose Edit in Audition, the audio renders into a new clip that is imported into Adobe Audition. When saved the clip is saved in Audition, the edited clip replaces the original clip in the Premiere Pro Timeline panel. The original master clip in the Project panel is untouched. Effects or markers applied to the original sequence clip are preserved in the edited clip.

- **Saving your multitrack session to different formats-** Although Audition allows you to save your files in many different formats, in most cases, you should save uncompressed audio to the AIFF or WAV formats. Save to the compressed mp3 format only when creating files for the web or portable media players.

- **Export multitrack mixdown files-** After you finish mixing a session, you can export all or part of it in a variety of common formats. When you export, the resulting file reflects current volume, pan, and effects settings routed to the Master track.
To quickly mix the entire audio down to a single track, use the choose

File > Export > Multitrack Mixdown> Entire Session.

- Right-click and Save As to download the <u>practice cleaning up audio files</u>

CLASS SEVEN HOMEWORK- 4 POINTS

1. Bring your flash drive

2. Right-click and choose Save As to download the <u>project files</u> and extract to your computer or flash drive

3. Follow the steps as listed below shown in the <u>video demonstration</u>

    a. Open Adobe Audition

    b. Change workspace to Edit Audio to Video

    c. Create a new Multitrack Session-Voice Over Commercial

    d. Import files

    e. Place video, music, voice over files onto tracks

    f. Reduce dB of pauses in voice over file

    g. Apply effect to voice over from Effects Rack>Track Effects> Radio Announcer Voice

    h. Add markers for effects where person kicks ball, lands after jump, throws football, and product is revealed

    i. Adjust Effects clip volumes

    j. Place stadium crowd onto track

    k. Trim stadium crowd sound

    l. Apply clip effect>analog delay>triplet refrain to Effect1

    m. Music track- fade out and fade in

    n. Save your project into the homework folder on your Flash drive

    o. Export the Multitrack mixdown as **class7.wav** into the same folder

    p. Navigate to the <u>Assignment page</u>

    q. Click on the **Submit Assignment** Button at the top of the Assignment page.

    r. Click the **Choose File** button and select your **class7.wav** file then click Open

    s. Click the **Submit Assignment** button.

CLASS EIGHT: ANIMATION BASICS

"Animation offers a medium of story telling and visual entertainment which can bring pleasure and information to people of all ages everywhere in the world."

— Walt Disney

WHAT IS ANIMATION?

Animation is the process of displaying still images in a rapid sequence to create the illusion of movement. These images can be hand drawn, computer generated, or pictures of 3D objects. Though most people associate animation with cartoons, it also has applications in industrial and scientific research.

CAREERS IN ANIMATION

Animators create animation and visual effects for films, video games, television, mobile devices, and other forms of media using illustrations and software programs. Animators also create graphics and develop storyboards, drawings and illustrations. They create, plan, and script animated narrative sequences, and assist with background design and production coordination. The Bureau of Labor Statistics (BLS) combines multimedia artists and animators into one career group. According to the Bureau, "multimedia artists and animators often work in a specific medium. Some focus on creating animated movies or video games. Others create visual effects for movies and television shows. Animators work in the motion picture and video industry, computer design and video gaming field, specializing in advertising, public relations campaigns, and much more. According to the BLS, the median annual wage for multimedia artists and animators was $61,370 in May 2012. The lowest 10 percent earned less than $34,860, and the top 10 percent earned more than $113,470.

The Bureau also mentions that a staggering 57 percent of animators were self-employed in 2012!

INTRODUCTION TO FLASH

Adobe Flash is a 2-D animation program that uses vector shapes and imported bitmap images to create simple and complex animations. Like films, Adobe Flash Professional documents divide lengths of time into frames. In the Timeline, you work with these frames to organize and control the content of your document. You place frames in the Timeline in the order you want the objects to appear in your finished content.

DRAWING IN FLASH

Flash allows you to create vector shapes or drawings that are small in file size. There are a variety of drawing tools that allow you to create lines, fills, brush strokes and shapes. Because of the way Flash handles shapes, clicking an outline only selects a section of the line, not the whole thing. Double-click a section of the stroke to select all connected sections at once.

EXPLORING THE FLASH INTERFACE

When you open Flash CC you will see the welcome screen. The welcome screen enables you to quickly open recent items, create a variety of new file types or new files from templates. You can also access various introductory videos and learning resources from this screen.

The Flash interface contains the following primary components:

1. The Stage where you will create vector artwork and manipulate animations.

2. The Timeline which helps you organize your content into layers and frames.

3. Multiple panels. Some examples of panels are the Properties panel, which contains information about the object that you have selected, and the Library, which stores the assets that you use in your Flash file. These assets can be imported bitmap graphics, sounds, video, or other reusable graphical elements.

4. The toolbar which enables you to create and manipulate artwork.

5. The menu which contains commands such as saving files, copying and pasting, and the help menu among others.

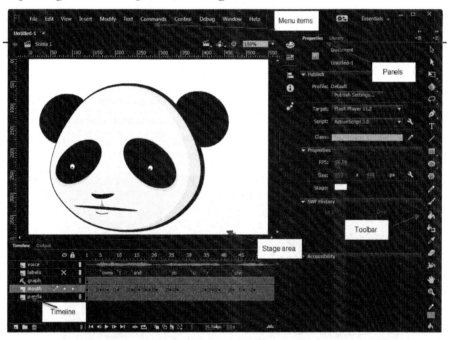

CLASS EIGHT HOMEWORK- 17 POINTS

1. Complete online midterm quiz (15 points)

2. Bring your flash drive

3. Watch Flash Professional CC- Click Get Started; watch videos listed under Essentials for beginners

4. Watch How to Create a Character Animation in Flash Professional

5. Select File> Save as **class8**.fla into **homework** folder on your Flash drive

6. Select File> Publish as **class8.swf** into the homework folder

7. Navigate to the Assignment page

8. Click on the **Submit Assignment** Button at the top of the Assignment page.

9. Click the **Choose File** button and select your **class8.swf** file then click Open

10. Click the **Submit Assignment** button. (2 points)

CLASS NINE: CREATING ANIMATIONS IN FLASH

BASIC FLASH ANIMATION CONCEPTS

FRAME RATES

The frame rate, the speed the animation is played at, is measured in number of frames per second (fps). A frame rate that's too slow makes the animation appear to stop and start; a frame rate that's too fast blurs the details of the animation. A frame rate of 24 fps is the default for new Flash documents and usually gives the best results on the web. The standard motion-picture rate is also 24 fps.

SYMBOLS AND INSTANCES

A symbol is a shape that you convert to a master copy which is stored in Flash's Library. You can then reuse the symbol throughout your document or in other documents. Using symbols in your documents dramatically reduces file size; saving several instances of a symbol requires less storage space than saving multiple copies of the contents of the symbol. A symbol can include artwork that you import from another application.

An instance is a copy of a symbol located on the Stage or nested inside another symbol. An instance can be different from its parent symbol in color, size, and function. Editing the symbol updates all of its instances, but applying effects to an instance of a symbol updates only that instance.

KEYFRAMES AND FRAMES

Keyframes are the foundation of animation dating back to early Disney Studio productions. Each frame consists of a drawing that is slightly altered from the one proceeding it. When you string enough of these together and play them quickly, you have animation. The speed at which they play is called the frame rate. In Flash a keyframe is a frame where a new object or symbol instance appears in the Timeline. A solid circle represents a keyframe with content on it, and an empty circle before the frame represents an empty keyframe. Subsequent frames added to the same layer have the same content as the keyframe. A keyframe can also be a frame that includes ActionScript code to control some aspect of your document. You can add a blank keyframe to the Timeline as a placeholder for symbols you plan to add later or to explicitly leave the frame blank.

- To create a new keyframe, select Insert > Timeline > Keyframe, or right-click (Windows) or Control-click (Macintosh) the frame where you want to place a keyframe, and select Insert Keyframe.

- To create a new blank keyframe, select Insert > Timeline > Blank Keyframe, or right-click (Windows) or Control-click (Macintosh) the frame where you want to place the keyframe, and select Insert Blank Keyframe.

- To delete a frame, keyframe, or frame sequence, select it and right-click (Windows) or Control-click (Macintosh) and select Remove Frames. Surrounding frames remain unchanged.

- To move a keyframe or frame sequence and its contents, select it and drag to the desired location.

- To extend the duration of a keyframe, Alt-drag (Windows) or Option-drag (Macintosh) it to the final frame of the new sequence.

- To change the length of a tweened sequence, drag the beginning or ending keyframe left or right.

- To reverse an animation sequence, select the appropriate frames in one or more layers and select Modify > Timeline > Reverse Frames. Keyframes must be at the beginning and end of the sequence.

FRAME-BY-FRAME ANIMATION

Frame-by-frame animation changes the contents of the Stage in every frame and is best suited to complex animation in which an image changes in every frame instead of simply moving across the Stage. Frame-by-frame animation increases file size more rapidly than tweened animation. In frame-by-frame animation, Flash stores the values for each complete frame.

To create a frame-by-frame animation, define each frame as a keyframe and create a different image for each frame. Each new keyframe initially contains the same contents as the keyframe preceding it, so you can modify the frames in the animation incrementally.

MOTION TWEENS

A motion tween is a quick and easy way to create animations in Flash. Where you specify different values for an object property in different frames. Flash calculates the values for that property in between those two frames. The term tween comes from the words "in between". You must convert shapes or imported bitmaps into symbols in order to create Motion Tweens.

For example, you can take a shape that you convert to a symbol and it left of the Stage in frame 1, and move it to the right of the Stage in frame 20. When you create a tween, Flash calculates all the positions of the movie clip in between. The result is an animation of the symbol moving from left to right, from frame 1 to frame 20. In each frame in between, Flash moves the movie clip one 20th of the distance across the Stage.

A tween span is a group of frames in the Timeline in which an object has one or more properties changed over time. A tween span appears in the Timeline as a group of frames in a single layer with a blue background. Only one object on the Stage can be animated in each tween span. Tweened animations allow you to create movement and property changes and minimize file size because the symbols used in the tween can be re-used without adding to the file size.

CLASSIC TWEENS

Classic tweens are an older way of creating animation in Flash. These tweens are similar to the newer motion tweens, but are more complicated to create and less flexible. However, classic tweens do provide some types of control over animation that motion tweens do not. In some situations, such as lip-syncing, classic tweens are still the best choice. Changes in a classic tween animation are defined in its keyframes. The "tween" or interpolated frames, appear as light blue or light green with an arrow drawn between keyframes.

SHAPE TWEENS

In shape tweening, you draw a shape at one specific frame in the Timeline, and change that shape or draw another shape at another specific frame. Flash then interpolates the intermediate shapes for the frames in between, creating the animation of one shape morphing into another. You can also tween the position and color of shapes within a shape tween.

The following steps show how to create a shape tween from frame 1 to frame 30 of the Timeline. However, you can create tweens in any part of the Timeline that you choose.

- In frame 1, draw a square with the Rectangle tool.

- Select frame 30 of the same layer and add a blank keyframe by choosing Insert > Timeline > Blank Keyframe or pressing F7.

- On the Stage, draw a circle with the Oval tool in frame 30. You should now have a keyframe in frame 1 with a square and a keyframe in frame 30 with a circle.

- In the Timeline, select one of the frames in between the two keyframes in the layer containing the two shapes.

- Choose Insert > Shape Tween. Flash interpolates the shapes in all the frames between the two keyframes.

- To preview the tween, scrub the playhead across the frames in the Timeline, or press the Enter key.

- To add easing to the tween, select one of the frames between the two keyframes and enter a value in the Ease field in the Property inspector.

- Enter a negative value to ease the beginning of the tween. Enter a positive value to ease the end of the tween.

PUBLISHING FLASH MOVIES

You can play Flash content in Internet browsers that are equipped with Flash Player, or inside stand-alone projectors, as well as with Active-X plug-ins. When creating and editing in Flash you are working with FLA files. When you use the Publish or Test Movie command, Flash creates a SWF file from your FLA file. By default, the Publish command creates a Flash SWF file and an HTML document that inserts your Flash content in a browser window. You can also publish the FLA file as GIFs, JPEGs, and PNGs —with the HTML needed to display them in the browser window. To test how the SWF file works before you publish your SWF file, use Test Movie (Control > Test Movie > Test) and Test Scene (Control > Test Scene).

CLASS NINE HOMEWORK- 4 POINTS

1. Bring your flash drive
2. Watch short "how to" videos on the following topics:
   a. Shape Tweens
   b. Motion Tweens
   c. Frame by frame animations
   d. Combining motion and shape tweens
3. Based on the instructions in the "Creating Basic Animations" file, create a similar project:
   a. Come up with a 5 second story to animate. Our practice story was a car driving along a road.
   b. Import the necessary clip art, or free draw your own content, to make your story work
   c. Convert your art into symbols for tweening purposes
   d. Create motion tweens that pan two or more background elements
   e. Create motion tweens that pan two foreground elements in the opposite direction of each other
   f. Create one frame-by-frame animation like the seagull demonstrated in the "Exploring Flash" class demonstration
4. Save your work as **class9.fla** into your homework folder
5. Select File> Publish. This will generate a file called **class9.swf**
6. Navigate to the Assignment page
7. Click on the **Submit Assignment** Button at the top of the Assignment page.
8. Click the **Choose File** button and select your **class9.swf** file then click Open
9. Click the **Submit Assignment** button.

CLASS TEN: GAME DEVELOPMENT WITH ACTIONSCRIPT SNIPPETS

CAREERS IN GAME DESIGN/DEVELOPMENT

Do you spend hours critiquing games on message boards or discussing how you'd improve them? Are you constantly daydreaming about creating them or coming up with your own stories and characters? Are you the type that writes fan fiction, draws characters, collects game art, or creates remixes of game music? Have you tried writing your own game design ideas, creating mods, or programming small flash games? But the field is highly competitive and successful game developers need a strong skill-set in art, math, and physics. The good news is that the pay is very good and the Bureau of Labor Statistics indicates that the game industry is continuing to grow at a very fast pace.

BASIC PROGRAMMING

When you look at the successful games over the years, they have compelling stories, beautiful artwork, awesome sound effects, and a team of incredibly talented people behind it all. A key player on the team is the programmer. Without the programmer you don't have the interactivity that makes the game feel like a personal experience. While there are many types of programming languages used in game development we are going to explore the basics of one that is used heavily in web-based games, ActionScript.

Want more information about the day in the life of a game developer? Watch the video here- https://www.youtube.com/watch?v=YrYs_9lEGyY

ACTIONSCRIPT PROGRAMMING BASICS

ActionScript is the object-oriented programming language used by Flash to create an interactive experience for users. It is very similar in its structure and syntax to JavaScript. Once you know one, the other will be easy to learn. Over the next few pages you will explore fundamental programming concepts that will help you understand the code you will use for the interactive game project you will be completing. These key terms and concepts apply to most programming languages.

VARIABLES

Variables are containers that hold different types of data; numbers, words, sounds, etc.

COMPARISON WITH FLASH STRUCTURE

- Symbols are containers for different objects you create in Flash
- Variables are containers you create with ActionScript
- They store the values of the different objects you create
- They can change dynamically

OBJECTS AND CLASSES

- Classes are the blueprint to define how objects behave.
- All objects are members of a Class and are instances of that Class.
- Example: Jeff is a member of the human class. Jeff is the object, and Human is the class. All objects within a class have a set of properties and methods (actions) that can be modified on an individual basis. Example: Hair is a property of the human class. Each object in the human class have different values associated with that property. These include hair color, straight, wavy, wiry hair, level of hairiness, etc.

PROPERTIES

- Properties are like adjectives; they describe objects
- Each class has a pre-defined set of properties.
- Each object of a class can have its own values set to its properties.
- Example; Movie Clip properties include: height, width, rotation
- You can define and change the properties of each object (instance) through ActionScript.

METHODS

- Methods are like verbs; the things objects can do
- Example; The Timeline is an object and has a gotoAndPlay() method. This method sends the timeline playhead to a specific location in the animation.
- When an object does something using a method we say the method is

called or that the object calls the method

CALLING A METHOD

The next step involves calling an object's methods or evaluating and assigning new properties. You can call a method by entering an expression using dot syntax. Example: In the example below we use the LOAD method to load a sound into the sound mixer. Sound is the class, load is the method, and nameOfSoundCreated is the variable name given to the sound.

```
sound.load(nameOfSoundCreated);
```

ACTIONSCRIPT SYNTAX

ActionScript uses dot syntax to put together objects, properties, and methods

Example;   movieclip1.   rotation   =   45

OBJECT   PROPERTY   VALUE

Methods are called in the same way

Example;   movie_clip.   gotoAndPlay   ("start")

　　　　　　OBJECT   METHOD   PARAMETER

The parenthesis after gotoAndPlay signifies a method rather than a property. The statement inside the parenthesis is an argument or a parameter

MORE PUNCTUATION

Semicolon functions as a period does in a sentence

Example:

```
stopAllSounds();
```

Curly braces group together related blocks of ActionScript statements

```
on (release) {
        stopAllSounds();
        play(); }
```

FUNCTIONS

CHARACTERISTICS OF FUNCTIONS

Functions hold actions and/or sets of actions. Functions allow you to control when they are run or executed.

Example: I have a video that plays within an animation but only when someone clicks on a button that says play. I would create the function but have it executed only when someone clicks on a button. The function is ready but is only called when needed.

FUNCTIONS FUNDAMENTALS

- Declaration- creating a function (remember- creating the function does NOT execute it
- Invocation- calling the function
- Arguments and parameters- providing the data to manipulate
- Termination- ending the execution

DECLARING A FUNCTION

Creating or declaring a function requires following the syntax indicated in the example below in which I create a function that sends the timeline to a specific frame label in the animation and stops all sounds that may have been playing in the animation until that point.

```
function home (event:MouseEvent): void
    {
        gotoAndStop ("home");;
        stopAllSounds();

    }
```

RUNNING OR INVOKING THE FUNCTION

One common way to invoke a function is to create a button, add an event listener and call the function.

```
home_btn.addEventListener (MouseEvent.CLICK, home);
```

In this example, a button named home_btn listens for a mouse click. Upon hear the click it runs a function called home. The function then goes to a frame within the animation and stops all sounds.

EVENTS, EVENT HANDLERS, AND EVENT LISTENERS

EVENTS

Events are things that happen while a Flash movie is playing. Many types of events exist, such as when a visitor to your Web site clicks a button, presses a key on the keyboard, or starts downloading a file. You can utilize events by running functions when events happen. The special functions that run when events happen are called event handlers.

EVENT HANDLERS

To write an event handler, create an event handler function. It receives information about the event that makes the function run.

EVENT LISTENERS

To attach an event to an event handler, use an event listener. Event listeners wait for events to happen, and invokes the appropriate event handler function. To invoke an event handler function use the addEventListener method. You type the instance name, type a dot, and type addEventListener. Then in parentheses, specify the type of event the instance is listening for, type a comma, and type the name of the function. For example, if you had a button with an instance name of btnPlay and you wanted to run a function called playMovie whenever you clicked it, you would type the following:

```
btnPlay.addEventListener (MouseEvent.CLICK,
playMovie);
```

ADDING INTERACTIVITY WITH CODE SNIPPETS

The Code Snippets panel in Flash enables non-programmers to quickly apply programming code to interactive projects without prior knowledge of JavaScript or ActionScript. With the Code Snippets panel, you can add code that affects the behavior of objects, controls the timeline, and allows touchscreen behaviors. Some code snippets require modification to fit the project needs. When you apply a code snippet, the code is added to the current frame of the Actions layer in the Timeline and adds an Action layer above all other layers in the Timeline.

To add a code snippet, you would:

• Select an object on the Stage or a frame in the Timeline.

• Open the Code Snippets panel (Window > Code Snippets) and double-click the snippet you want to apply.

• In the Actions panel, view the newly added code and replace any necessary items according to the instructions at the top of the snippet.

SOUNDS AND FLASH

Adobe Flash Professional offers several ways to use sound; make sounds that play continuously, independent of the Timeline, or use the Timeline to synchronize animation to a sound track, add sounds to buttons to make them more interactive, and make sounds fade in and out for a more polished sound track.

There are two types of sounds in Flash Professional: event sounds and stream sounds. An event sound must download completely before it begins playing, and it continues playing until explicitly stopped. Stream sounds begin playing as soon as enough data for them has loaded. Streaming sounds are most appropriate for lip-syncing because as you drag the playhead through the timeline you can hear the sound playing while watching your animation.

CLASS TEN HOMEWORK- 4 POINTS

Right-click and Save As to download the Art Heist game. Then open it in Flash and follow the instructions

CREATING A SIMPLE GAME WITH CODE SNIPPETS

Adapted from "Creating a simple mobile game using the Code Snippets panel in Flash" by Yuki Shimizu

The Code Snippets panel contains ActionScript 3 snippets that are commonly used in many Flash projects, including banner advertisements and games. The following code snippets are featured in this tutorial:

• Click and Drag Event

• Mouse Over Event

• Countdown Timer

• Stop At This Frame

• Click To Go To Frame And Stop

The premise of the game is to steal the Cezanne paintings from the museum without touching the moving security laser beams. There are three frames in the game's FLA document. The first frame contains the game's instructions, the second frame contains the game's graphics and play logic, and the third frame contains the "Game Over" screen.

The first task involves adding code snippets to the game instruction screen on Frame 1 so that the instructions are displayed when the game first loads (see Figure 1). It's necessary to add the code to this section (Frame 1) because otherwise the playhead would immediately move on to Frame 2 and skip over the game instructions.

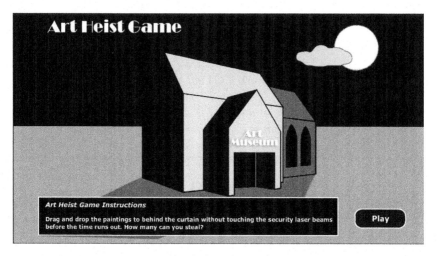

Figure 1. When the game first loads, the Game Instructions screen is displayed.

PAUSING ON FRAME 1 WITH "STOP AT THIS FRAME"

Insert the code that pauses the playhead at Frame 1 (the frame that contains the game instructions) so that users have a chance to read the instructions before clicking the Play button:

1. Locate and open the ArtHeist_start.fla file.

2. Click Frame 1 of the instruction layer to position the playhead on Frame 1 (the game instruction screen) in the Timeline.

3. Choose Window > Code Snippets to open the Code Snippets panel and see the list of code snippets organized in different categories.

4. Open the Timeline Navigation category and double-click the "Stop at this Frame" snippet. The Actions panel opens to show that the stop(); command is added.

Notice that the Actions layer is automatically created above the other layers in the Timeline and the code is added to Frame 1 of this layer. All of the code snippets you insert will be added to this layer going forward.

UPDATING THE PLAY BUTTON FUNCTIONALITY WITH "CLICK TO GO TO FRAME AND STOP"

Here you'll add the code to make the Play button go to Frame 2 when it's clicked:

1. Click Frame 1 in the Actions layer of the Timeline to ensure that the playhead is still positioned on Frame 1.

2. Select the movie clip symbol of the Play button that appears on the Stage.

3. In the Code Snippets panel, double-click the Click to Go to Frame and Stop snippet in the Timeline Navigation category. Flash displays a notification to let you know that you need to supply an instance name. Click Cancel and go to the Properties panel and assign the instance name Play_MC (see Figure 2).

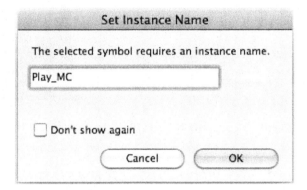

Then go back to the Code Snippets panel, double-click the Click to Go to Frame and Stop snippet in the Timeline Navigation category.

4. The Actions panel opens and shows that the snippet is inserted. In this sample project, the goal is to move the playhead to Frame 2 when the user clicks the play button. Therefore, change the last line in the sample code from gotoAndStop (5); to gotoAndStop (2); The value in the parentheses indicates the frame number. Note: There are multiple ways to accomplish the same goal in Flash. In the video demonstration I use the approach of Click to go to Next Frame and Stop.

5. Choose Control > Test Movie > Test to test the FLA file. When the file plays in Flash Player, confirm that the game instructions (Frame 1) is displayed and paused. When you click the Play button, the playhead moves to the area with the game's logic (Frame 2).

ADDING THE GAME FUNCTIONALITY

In this section you will add code to Frame 2, which contains the graphics and code that enable users to play the game. Frame 2 contains graphics that simulate the inside of the museum and pedestals that each display a precious gem. The object of the game is to swipe the gems without touching the moving laser beams (see Figure 3).

Figure 3. The Stage on Frame 2 contains the graphics that make up the game.

UPDATING THE PAINTINGS WITH THE CLICK AND DRAG EVENT SNIPPET

Here you'll add the Click and Drag Event code snippet, which makes it possible for game players to use their mouse to select and drag the paintings. To steal the paintings, players must touch and drag the paintings to position them behind the red curtain:

1. The two snippets that you added in the previous section are already added to this file.

2. In the Timeline, click Frame 2 in the Actions layer.

3. Select the first painting on the stage. It is already named Painting1_ MC.

4. Choose Window > Code Snippets to open the Code Snippets panel, if it is closed.

5. Open the Actions category and double-click the "Drag and Drop" snippet. The Actions panel opens and shows that the snippet is added.

6. Repeat Steps 3–5 for the Painting2_MC and the Painting3_MC movie clip symbols.

UPDATING THE LASER BEAMS WITH THE "MOUSE OVER EVENT" SNIPPET

Frame 2 contains three laser beams that move when you test the movie. When the mouse intersects with any of the laser beams, the playhead should jump to Frame 3, which displays the Game Over screen:

1. Click Frame 2 to ensure that the playhead of the Timeline is still on Frame 2.

2. Select the middle laser (red line). Notice its Instance name in the Properties panel is Laser1_MC.

3. Choose Window > Code Snippets to open the Code Snippets panel, if it is closed.

4. Open the Event Handlers category and double-click the "Mouse Over Event" snippet. The Actions panel opens and shows that the snippet is added.

5. Repeat Steps 2–4 to apply the snippet to the Laser2_MC and Laser3_MC symbols.

6. REPLACE CODE: Read the instructions for the Mouse Over Event snippet in the Actions panel carefully. The code example below is set to display the words "Moused over" in the Output panel:

```
// Start your custom code

// This example code displays the words "Moused over"
in the Output panel.

trace("Moused over");

// End your custom code
```

Instead of tracing a text message, the goal here is to jump the playhead to Frame 3 when a player accidentally touches one of the laser beams.

Edit the code for all three Lasers.

Remove the entire section

```
// Start your custom code

// This example code displays the words "Moused over"
in the Output panel.

trace("Moused over");

// End your custom code
```

and replace it with

```
gotoAndStop (3);
```

Test your movie again. If you have any error messages you need to check your code for spelling or case errors.

DEFINING THE DURATION OF THE COUNTDOWN TIMER SNIPPET

You can add a simple timer to this game with the Countdown Timer code snippet. One of the aspects of this sample game is that users only have 10 seconds to steal the gems and play the game. When the time has elapsed, the playhead jumps to Frame 3, which displays the "Game Over" message. Follow the steps below to add and update the Countdown Timer code snippet:

1. In the Timeline, click Frame 2 of the Actions layer to set the location of the playhead.

2. If the Code Snippets panel is not already open, choose Window > Code Snippets to open it. Scroll down to the bottom of the Actions category and double-click the Countdown Timer snippet. The Actions panel opens and shows that the snippet is added. This snippet counts down from a specified number of seconds, which is set at 10,000 milliseconds (10 seconds). By default, the timer counts down each second (10, 9, 8, and so on) and displays the remaining number of seconds in the output panel.

Copy the code below:

```
function fl_CountDownTimerHandler_3(event:
TimerEvent): void {

    if (fl_SecondsToCountDown_3 == 1) {

        gotoAndStop(3);

        fl_SecondsToCountDown_3 = 0;

    } else {

        fl_SecondsToCountDown_3--;

    }

}
```

Select the code below in the Actions panel and paste your copied code from above to replace the selected code:

```
function fl_
CountDownTimerHandler_3(event:TimerEvent):void

{

    trace(fl_SecondsToCountDown_3 + " seconds");

    fl_SecondsToCountDown_3--;

}
```

After making this change, 10 seconds after the play button is clicked, the game will display the Game Over message even if the user didn't intersect or touch any of the security laser beams.

Test your movie once again.

DISPLAYING THE "GAME OVER" SCREEN

UPDATING THE PLAY AGAIN BUTTON TO ADD THE "CLICK TO GO TO FRAME AND STOP" SNIPPET

The first task involves adding code that causes the playhead to jump to Frame 2 when the user clicks the Play Again button:

1. In the Timeline, click Frame 3 of the Actions layer to set the location of the playhead.

2. Select the movie clip symbol named PlayAgain_MC on the stage.

3. In the Code Snippets panel select the Timeline Navigation category, double-click the "Click to Go to Frame and Stop" snippet.

4. The Actions panel opens and shows that the snippet is inserted. The goal is to move the playhead to Frame 2 when the user clicks the Play Again button.

5. Locate and edit this line from this:
   `gotoAndStop(5);`   to this: `gotoAndStop(2);`

This change enables the player to start a new game. When they click the Play Again button, the playhead jumps to Frame 2. This displays the Stage with the paintings so that the user can try to steal them again.

ACCESSING MORE GAMES

1. In the Timeline, click Frame 3 of the Actions layer to set the location of the playhead.

2. Select the movie clip symbol named More Games on the Stage. Look at the Property inspector while the symbol instance is selected and notice that the instance name is set to More_MC.

3. Select the Actions category of code Snippets and double-click on "Click

to Go to Web Page"

4. In the line of code that says "navigateToURL(new URLRequest ("http://www.adobe.com"), "_blank"); replace http://www.adobe.com with a gaming website of your choice

SWAPPING OUT THE PAINTINGS

1. Go to a search engine and type in Paintings

2. When the search results appear click the Images link

3. Right-click on three images of your choice and choose Save image as, and save them to your computer

4. Open Flash and choose File> Import to Library

5. Import your three items

6. Select the Library panel and double-click on the Painting1_MC symbol

7. Select the painting on the Symbol's stage and delete it

8. Drag one of your imported bitmap images from the Library and place it with its center point on the cross-hairs of the Symbols stage

9. Select the Library panel and double-click on the Painting2_MC symbol and repeat steps 7 and 8

10. Select the Library panel and double-click on the Painting3 symbol and repeat steps 7 and 8

SAVING THE GAME

1. Select File> Save As and name the file **class10.fla** into the homework folder on your Flash drive or cloud storage drive

2. Select File> Publish settings. The name in the Output file window should be **class10.swf**

3. Click on the Select Publish Destination Folder icon and choose the homework folder of your flash drive.

4. Click Publish and OK.

5. Navigate to the Assignment page

6. Click on the **Submit Assignment** Button at the top of the Assignment page.

7. Click the **Choose File** button and select your **class10.swf** file then click Open

8. Click the **Submit Assignment** button. (4 points)

CLASS ELEVEN: VIDEO AND PREMIERE PRO FUNDAMENTALS

VIDEO STORYTELLING

Video is a natural medium for storytelling and has been the cornerstone of storytelling since its advent in the 1950s. Video is among the most powerful and most popular storytelling tools. Every month, more than 200 BILLION videos are viewed on personal and professional websites, video channels, social media sites and blogs. Well-made videos have the power to engage an audience, showcase a product, describe a concept and generate a call to action.

WHAT IS VIDEO PRODUCTION?

According to Wikipedia, video production is the "process of creating video by capturing moving images (videography), and creating combinations and reductions of parts of this video in live production and post-production (video editing)." In practical terms, video production varies from video creation to video editing in a variety of situations. Video production plays a role in television, corporate events, marketing, real estate, training, and many more fields.

VIDEO PRODUCTION CAREERS

If you love to tell stories and have a knack working with lights, cameras, and action this might be a career for you. The field of video production includes careers for lighting technicians, camera operators, cinematographers (they orchestrate the vision of the project), film editors, producers, and directors. The U.S. Bureau of Labor Statistics (BLS) reported the median earnings for camera operators was $43,390, video and film editors as $51,300 in May 2012, while producers and directors made a median salary of $71,350 across all industries (film, video, radio, television and stage).

You will be exploring the world of video editing using Adobe Premiere. While there are many very powerful video editing tools, Premiere is one of the few that is available for both Mac and Windows operating systems.

VIDEO AND PREMIERE PRO FUNDAMENTALS

The steps you take in editing video using Premiere Pro or any other non-linear video editing are similar. From import or capture through final output, the post-production video editing workflow process is described below.

DEFINING YOUR STORY

The essence of any project is the story you want to tell. From storyboarding to writing a complete screenplay, it is important that you have a good idea of the message you want to convey.

ASSEMBLE YOUR ASSETS

These include video clips, images, sounds, backgrounds, and anything else that supports your story's vision.

STARTING OR OPENING A PROJECT

If you are starting a new project, the New Project dialog launches. Here you can specify the name and location of the project file, the video capture format, and other settings for your project. After you have chosen settings in the New Project dialog, click OK. After you have exited the New Project dialog, the New Sequence dialog will appear. Choose the sequence preset in the dialog that matches the settings of your footage. Name the sequence at the bottom of the dialog, and then click OK.

ASSEMBLE AND EDIT A SEQUENCE

You can use the Source Monitor to view clips, set edit points, and mark other important frames before adding clips to a sequence. You add clips to a sequence in a Timeline panel by dragging them there or by using the Insert or Overwrite buttons in the Source Monitor.

ADD TITLES

The Titler Tool creates still titles, title rolls, or title crawls that you can easily superimpose over video. You can also access pre-built title templates.

ADD TRANSITIONS AND EFFECTS

The Effects panel includes an extensive list of transitions and effects you can apply to clips in a sequence. You can adjust these effects using the Effect Controls panel. The Effect Controls panel also lets you animate a clip's properties using traditional keyframing techniques.

MIX AUDIO

The Audio Track Mixer emulates a full-featured audio mixing board, complete with fade and pan sliders, sends, and effects. Premiere Pro saves your adjustments in real time.

EXPORT

Using Adobe Media Encoder, you can customize settings for MPEG-2, MPEG-4, FLV, and other formats, to the needs of your viewing audience.

SETTING UP A PREMIERE PRO PROJECT

The first step in any Premiere video production is setting up a new project. As I indicated when you worked with Adobe Audition, it is ESSENTIAL that you keep all your support files organized in a project folder when working on a project. These files are not embedded in the project and you need those files for the duration of the project. Starting the project with your files organized in one master folder for each project is a big time saver.

Within the New Project dialog box it is crucial that you save the project file in the same location as the files you are using. In other words, save the file in the master folder for each project as mentioned above.

Once inside the new project you still have several steps before you can really get down to work. You need to create a sequence within which you will import your assets; images, sounds, and video clips, for editing.

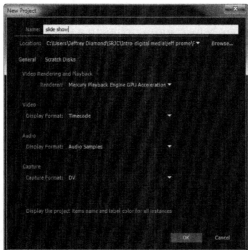

First step is to select **New Sequence** from the File menu. Once the new sequence has been created, you can choose your sequence settings. In general, the settings of a sequence should match those of the primary footage type in the sequence. Though Premiere Pro can mix footage of various types in a sequence and compensate for differences in characteristics, performance and quality are maximized when such conversions are avoided. In the case of the screen shot below I am using a Sequence Preset assuming I have footage shot with a Canon Rebel camera recorded in 1280 x 720 pixels.

PREMIERE PRO INTERFACE

Once you click OK to the new sequence you will see the Premiere Pro workspace. A typical workflow involves importing assets into the Project panel, and selecting them and placing them into the timeline. Then you can cut, adjust clips, add and edit transitions and effects between and on clips using built-in effects and editing effects with the Effects Control panel. The Preview panel allows you to view the project within the Premiere authoring environment.

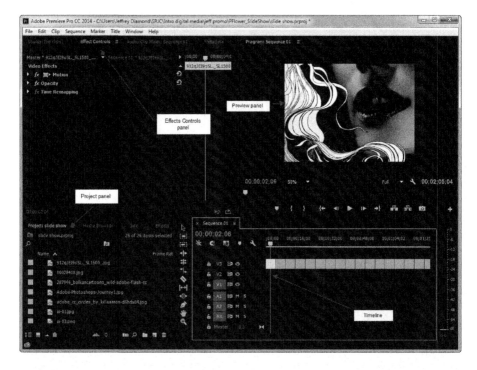

Download the files here to create a practice slide show in class

CLASS ELEVEN HOMEWORK- 5 POINTS

1. Bring your flash drive

2. Watch Premiere Pro CC Tutorials

   a. Essential for beginners- Overview of the Interface, Import media, Edit to the timeline, Add transitions, Add and adjust titles, Add and adjust the music, and Export video from Premiere Pro.

3. **Create a 1-2 minute slide show in Premiere- 4 points**
   Watch the instructional video that demonstrates this process
   Project Requirements:

   a. Your Slide Show must include a minimum of 10 bitmap images (jpgs or pngs) at a resolution of 72 ppi. Their size should be no less than 1000 pixels in width. The best source for your images would be your own collection or http://images.google.com.

   b. At least one background audio clip no longer than the length of your project.

   c. A fade in and fade out effect on your audio file.

   d. Title Text.

   e. A color Matte with a lighting effect

   f. At least two different filmmaking techniques including but not limited to pans, zooms, fades, cross-fades, tilts, rotations, etc. See the video transitions for ideas.

4. Project Instructions:

   a. Create new folder on your desktop called slide_show

   b. Collect and place 10 of your own images, and an audio background accompaniment into the slide_show folder

   c. Save your Premiere movie as **class11.pproj** into the slide_show folder on your desktop

   d. In Premiere select> Export> Media

   e. In the Export Settings Dialog box select Format: H.264, Output: Medium Bitrate

   f. In the Output Name field click on the underlined text and save as **class11.mp4**

   g. Choose your **class11.mp4** file into your homework folder (4 points)

   h. Exit Premiere

    i.   Move the entire slide_show folder into the homework folder of your Intro to Digital Media folder on your flash drive or upload it to the cloud storage device you have chosen to use.

5. **Write a short speech for upcoming video resume- 1 point**

    a.   Using any text editing program, write a 45-60 second speech that highlights your strengths and interests related to digital media. Try to memorize it, practice in front of a mirror. You might want to increase font size to 36 points so you can tape it to the bottom of the camera and make it easy to read in case you do not memorize the speech.

    b.   Example of content you should have in your speech:

    c.   Hi. My name is _____

    d.   I've been interested in digital media for (specify your area of interest)

    e.   I have experience with name the digital media tools you have used

    f.   My latest interests are in name your areas if interest

    g.   Mention your past work experiences

    h.   Mention being a good team player, hard worker, flexible, and willing to try new things

    i.   Summarize what you said and say thank you.

    j.   Here is a link to a video resume sample to get ideas what to write

6. Copy the text of your speech for pasting later

7. Save your speech to your homework folder

8. Navigate to the Assignment page

9. Click on the **Submit Assignment** Button at the top of the Assignment page.

10. Click the **Choose File** button and select your **class11.mp4** file then click Open

11. Click the Text Entry tab on the Assignment page

12. Paste your speech into the text entry field

13. Click the **Submit Assignment** button.

COME PREPARED TO SPEAK IN FRONT OF THE CAMERA. DRESS NICELY. DO NOT WEAR **GREEN**. PREFERABLE COLORS ARE RED, AND OTHER NON-SKIN TONE COLORS. AVOID STRIPES AND PATTERNS.

CLASS TWELVE: VIDEO POST-PRODUCTION WITH PREMIERE

CHROMA KEY COMPOSITING

Chroma key compositing, or chroma keying, is a special effects/post-production technique for compositing (layering) two images or video streams together based on color hues (chroma range). The technique has been used heavily in many fields to remove a background from the subject of a photo or video – particularly the newscasting, motion picture and videogame industries. The chroma keying technique is commonly used in video production and post-production. Green and blue backgrounds are commonly used because they differ most distinctly in hue from most human skin colors. No part of the subject being filmed or photographed may duplicate a color used in the background.

PREMIERE PRO ULTRA KEY EFFECT

The Ultra Key in Premiere Pro is a way of quickly and efficiently 'Green/Blue Screening' or 'Chroma Keying' footage elements shot against a colored background. There are several steps one must follow to successfully use this effect.

Once you apply the Ultra Key effect you must choose the clip in the timeline to which you applied the effect. Then select the eyedropper tool and click on the color you want to "key out". There are a variety of modifications we will explore in class with this tool.

CLASS TWELVE HOMEWORK

1. Download your video clip from the class website
2. Download a free video background loop from the class website
3. Create or import an audio background mix for your resume.
4. Come to class with your background, music file, any other assets (product shots, your own photography, etc.) to begin assembly of your final product.

CLASS THIRTEEN: IMPORTING, COMPOSITING, AND EXPORTING VIDEO

We have been working with various multimedia program up until now but we have yet to integrate several software applications in the same project. Most digital media professionals will use two to four applications in a single project. We will use both Premiere Pro and Adobe Audition to master our video resume.

CLASS THIRTEEN HOMEWORK- 10 POINTS

Watch the <u>instructional video</u> that demonstrates the steps below

1. Create new folder on your desktop called resume

2. Collect and place ALL your asset (product shots, background music, backgrounds, images)

3. Start new Premiere project and save as **resume.pproj** into the resume folder. *PPROJ is the file type associated with the project. It is NOT a video and does NOT get uploaded at the conclusion of this assignment.*

4. Select File> New Sequence> Mobile & Devices> iPod, etc. Then choose Settings. Adjust the Timebase to 29.97 frames/second. Change the name of the sequence to **resume**, and click OK.

5. Select File> New Title and create an opening title that fades in from black

6. Select File> Import and import your video clip, backgrounds, product shots, background music files, etc.

7. Place opening title and your video clip on the timeline

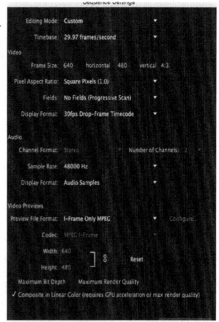

8. Reduce background noise from speech audio track in Audition

   a. Right-click on the Audio track in Premiere Pro, choose Edit Clip in Adobe Audition

   b. Use the Marquee Tool to select an area of background sound in the Audio file

   c. Use keyboard shortcut Shift + P to create a noise sample

   d. Use keyboard shortcut G to de-select the sample

   e. Use keyboard short Control + Shift + P to apply the noise reduction process

   f. Save the file and return to Premiere Pro

9. Key out the green screen- Click and drag the Ultra Key from the Effects panel onto your video clip

10. Use the eyedropper and select the green screen close to the subject

11. Change the Ultra Key Setting from Default to Aggressive, adjust Matte Generation appropriately; reduce highlight and shadow settings, increase pedestal.

12. Edit your speech by cutting unnecessary parts using the Razor tool

13. Create a lower third- in CC import from Adobe Premiere Pro CS6, Presets, Templates, Lower Thirds

14. Create and use a closing credits

15. Place ambient background audio on timeline and adjust the length to fit the rest of the timeline content. Use Exponential Fade for beginning and end. NOTE: Make sure the volume of the background audio is VERY low compared to the speaking voice!

16. Create smooth transitions between all scenes and objects (use Video Transition Effects)

17. In Premiere select> **Export> Media**

18. In the Export Settings Dialog box select **Format: H.264, Output: Medium Bitrate**

19. In the Output Name field click on the underlined text and save your movie as **resume.mp4** into the resume folder. *NOTE: Do NOT upload the PPROJ file type.*

20. Exit Premiere

21. Navigate to the <u>Assignment page</u>

22. Click on the **Submit Assignment** Button- top of the Assignment page.

23. Click the **Choose File** button, select **resume.mp4** and click Open

24. Click the **Submit Assignment** button. (10 points)

CLASS FOURTEEN: WEB DEVELOPER BASICS

We have spent the better part of this semester creating stories with images, illustrations, audio, animations, and videos. Now we have arrived at the time where we organize and display the fruits of our labor where everyone can see it; the worldwide web.

CAREERS IN WEB DEVELOPMENT AND DESIGN

Web designers and developers are the people responsible for creating and maintaining websites. A typical project includes meeting with clients to understand their goals and objectives, designing and-redesigning a website according to their desires, writing the code, adding multimedia, checking for bugs and fixing them, and "rolling out" the website to the client before going "live".

Some Web developers will work in Photoshop to create the overall design, while others will be in charge of writing the code in programming languages such as HTML and CSS. Still others on a typical web team will be developing the back-end programming that adds the dynamic and data-driven elements of the website. Web designers and developers need a thorough understanding of software programs, web applications and programming languages and a solid understanding of design principles. Work environments for Web developers vary from large corporations or governments to small businesses.

The Bureau of Labor Statistics projects about 20 percent employment growth for Web developers by 2022. Increased reliance on mobile devices is another reason the industry's employment growth should remain strong. Since June 2012 the percentage of web pages viewed on tablets has grown from 0 to 20%. This doesn't even take into account the amount of content people are viewing with their Smartphones or the number of apps people are using which is not counted as web page views. The BLS reports that Web developers made a median salary of $63,160 in 2013. The highest-paid in the profession earned $110,350, while the lowest-paid earned $33,320 that year. Computer systems design and information services employ the largest share of Web developers in the field. Web developers will continue to be in high demand and must continually update their skills to respond to changes in technology.

Job titles in the web industry include:

- Web Designer- The design specialist who also has a fundamental knowledge of HTML, CSS, and light JavaScript.
- Front End Developer- This job focuses on HTML, CSS, JavaScript, and light back-end work, not design.
- UX Designer- UX Designers focus on studying and researching how people use a site. May not have or need any design or implementation skill. They work very closely with
- UI/Interaction Designer- These folks take the results of the UX research and create and re-create the site design. This iterative process is ongoing. UI Designers must be experts with their design-tools-of-choice with perhaps only light HTML and CSS skill.
- Web/Back-end Developer- This job is focused on back end work and working with languages specific to the web, like PHP, ASP, Ruby, Python, etc. They usually have some knowledge of JavaScript and HTML. This is very different from a Front End Developer as there is little working with the design and primary focus on programming.
- SEO Specialist- Search Engine Optimization (SEO) Specialist's main role is to analyze, review and implement changes to websites so they are optimized for search engines.

Watch this to get a sense of a day in the life of a web designer/developer
https://www.youtube.com/watch?v=mlfSZChro8E

SET UP AN ACCOUNT ON STUDENT.SANTAROSA.EDU

1. Set up a web account at https://student.santarosa.edu:85/apply/linux-account.php

2. Go to http://student.santarosa.edu/Student_pswd.html for password information.
   Your default password is your initials capitalized and the last 5 of your student ID.

3. Write down this information below. You will need it for the duration of the semester.

4. Need review? Watch the video here

SET UP YOUR WEB PAGE DIRECTORY (WINDOWS)

1. From off-campus- Download and install SSH Secure Shell Client

2. Launch SSH Secure Shell Client in the SSH Secure folder from the Start menu.

3. Click the Connect icon in the top of the window

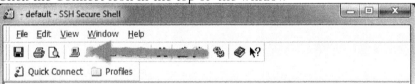

4. Fill out the Connect to Remote Host dialog box, using Your User Name, click Connect

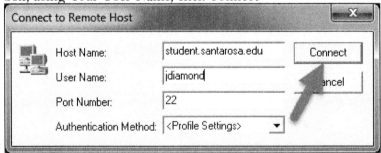

5. Enter your password and click OK.

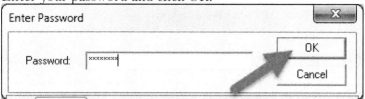

6. Type sudo wwwme and press Enter.

7. Your directory will be created and your path will be shown on screen.

8. Write down- /home/WWW_pages/yourusername
   This will be the Host Directory you use in your Dreamweaver site definition.

9. Exit SSH Secure Shell Client and Disconnect.

SET UP YOUR WEB PAGE DIRECTORY (MAC OSX)

1. Open up a Terminal (under Applications find Utilities; Terminal should be in there)

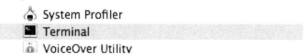

2. Type "ssh your-user-name@student.santarosa.edu" (i.e.: John Smith would type ssh jsmith@student.santarosa.edu). NOTE: There is a space after ssh.

3. Type sudo wwwme at the command line and hit the Return key. NOTE: There is a space between sudo and wwwme

4. Your directory will be created and your path will be shown on screen.

5. Write down-- /home/WWW_pages/yourusername
This will be the Host Directory you use in your Dreamweaver site definition.

CLASS FOURTEEN HOMEWORK- 2 POINTS

1. Bring your Flash Drive!
2. Make sure your website is functioning
   a. Open any web browser
   b. In the URL address bar type
      student. santarosa.edu/~yourusername/
   c. You should see either content from other classes you are taking that required a website or something similar to the picture here showing your username

Index of /~jdiamond

Name	Last modified	Size	Description

 Parent Directory   -

   d. If you see FILE NOT FOUND you will need to watch the video on setting up your student.santarosa.edu account and website.

DEFINE A SITE WITH DREAMWEAVER

Watch this video COMPLETELY before trying to set up your site

DOWNLOAD WEBSITE FILES

1. Right-click and Save As to download the website start files
2. Extract them and place them in your **intro_digital_media** folder. Note: Do not change the names of the files or folders.
3. Launch Dreamweaver
4. Watch the instructional video again and take the quiz at the end.
5. Complete ALL the steps in the video. Note: As per the video, the path to your files on the student server MUST be

   student.santarosa.edu/~yourname/intro_digital_media

   in order for the website to work properly for this class.

DEFINE YOUR SITE IN DREAMWEAVER CC

1. Launch Dreamweaver

2. Select Site> New Site

3. Fill in the Site Name with the name of your class Intro to Digital Media- Your Name.

4. For Local Site Folder click the browse for folder icon to the right of the text field and point to the intro_digital_media sub-folder you created on your Flash drive.

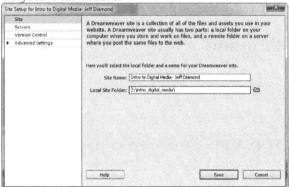

5. Select the Servers category

   a. Click the + sign below the white dialog box

   b. In the Server Name field type Student Server

   c. In the Connect Using field select the drop down arrow and change FTP to SFTP

   d. In the SFTP Address text field type in student.santarosa.edu

   e. In the Username text field type in your username

f. In the Password text field type in your password

g. Click on Test. This should say you have successfully connected.

h. In the Root Directory field type in /home/WWW_pages/ yourusername

i. In the Web URL field type http:// student.santarosa.edu/~youruserrname/

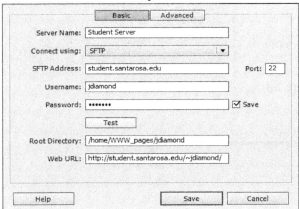

j. Click Save.

k. Click OK.

l. Click Done.

6. Create a new Remote sub-directory

a. Select the drop down menu indicated by the arrow in the Files Panel

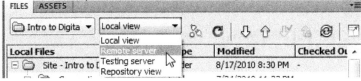

b. Choose Remote Server

c. Click on the Plug icon to connect to the Remote Server

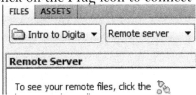

d. Right click (Mac--Ctrl-click) on Root folder of Remote site and select New Folder.

e. Click New Folder to create it and then rename it-- intro_digital_
   media *NOTE: The name must be EXACT in order to connect to your web
   site.*

f. In the Files panel select the arrow next to your site definition and

   choose Manage Sites.

g. Select Edit.

h. Select the Servers category.

i. Double-click on Student Server

j. Add **intro_digital_media** to the end of your Root Directory and to
   the end of the Web URL names. Note the tilde (~) in the Web URL
   after your name

| Root Directory: | /home/WWW_pages/jdiamond/intro_digital_media |
| Web URL: | http://student.santarosa.edu/~jdiamond/intro_digital_media |

k. Click Test and click Save.

7. Set up a Testing Server

a. With the Servers category still open click on the duplicate icon at
   the bottom of the server definition window

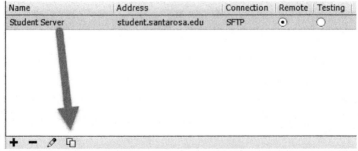

b. Click Save. Your server definition should look like this.

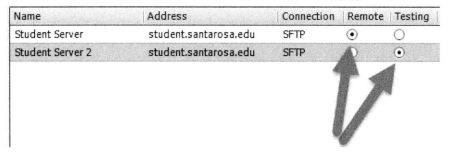

CHECK AND UPLOAD YOUR WEB PAGES

1. Make sure you are inside your site definition. You should see the site name at the top right of the Files panel. It should look like the screen shot you see here.

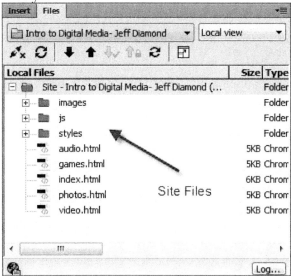

2. Select **site folder** in the Files panel

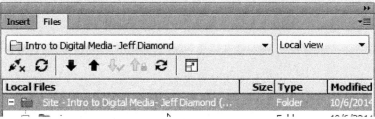

3. Click on the **up arrow**

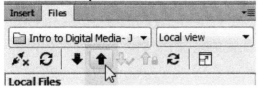

4. When asked if you are sure if you want to upload the entire site click OK.

5. Launch a web browser and in the address bar at the top of the browser window, type in

   `http://student.santarosa.edu/~yourusername/intro_`
   `digital_media/index.html.`

6. Make sure that your page appears in the web browser.

7. Select and copy the URL in the address bar

SEND ME THE LINK TO YOUR PAGE

1. Navigate to the Assignment page

2. Click on the **Submit Assignment** Button at the top of the Assignment page.

3. Copy your **website link** into the Website URL text field and click the **Submit Assignment** button.

Export/Import Site Definitions allows easy access to site definitions.

1. Select Site> Manage Sites> and click on the **Export** icon near the bottom left corner of the Manage Sites window With the Back up my settings button selected click OK and save your settings to your site's local root folder. This will create a small text file with all your settings.

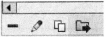

2. Close Dreamweaver

Importing Site Settings (NOTE: To be done **only once** when working on your own computer and every time you use a computer that does not show your site definition)

1. Open Dreamweaver

2. Import your defined settings by selecting Site> Manage Sites>Import Site.

3. Select your site definition file and click OK. You are ready to work.

Working in the SRJC lab

1. Always use flash drives in the SRJC labs for your work.

2. Define your site with the local root folder pointing to your flash drive.

CLASS FIFTEEN: WEB DEVELOPMENT AND THE DREAMWEAVER INTERFACE

Now that we have set up our websites let's learn the basics of the markup and programming languages used to create websites and explore Adobe Dreamweaver. Dreamweaver will enable us to focus on the design-side of website development and the code side if we are interested in a more in-depth understanding.

WEB DEVELOPMENT LANGUAGES

1. HTML (Hypertext Markup Language) is a standardized system for tagging text files to achieve font, color, graphic, and hyperlink effects on World Wide Web pages. HTML is responsible for the structure of the webpage. A properly structured webpage is more likely to rank high when searching for web content with search engines such as Google or Bing.

2. CSS (Cascading Style Sheets) provide an easy way to control appearance of a web page or site. Changes made to one external style sheet can affect multiple pages linked to that external style sheet. The primary purpose is to separate presentation of the page from its structure.

   a. Great examples of implementing CSS presentation to a page's structure can be seen at http://www.zengarden.com

3. JavaScript is an object-oriented computer programming language commonly used to create interactive effects within web browsers.

DREAMWEAVER BASICS

SETTING UP YOUR WORKSPACE

You can control Dreamweaver's layout by selecting Window> Workspace layout. In our class we will be using DESIGN view. This is very important because **Design** view includes the **Properties** panel at the bottom of the document window.

THE WELCOME SCREEN

Gives you quick access to many options including Create: New, Recent Files, Starter Templates, New Features, Getting Started, and Tips & Techniques.

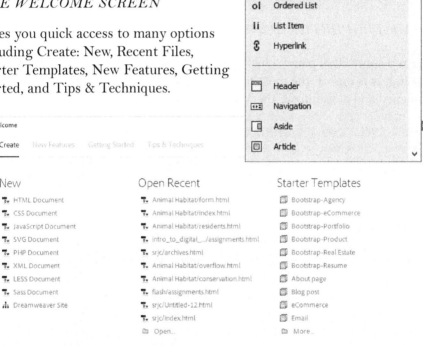

You can turn the Welcome Screen on and off from the Tips & Techniques tab of the Welcome screen and the Preferences.

THE INSERT BAR

Contains icons for all the actions you need. There are many sub-menus or additional tabs included with the Insert bar. You can control if the Insert bar appears with Menu items or Tabs by selecting Options from right corner of the Insert bar. The Files panel shows up next to it in Design view. The Files panel is important for site and file management

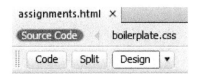

THE PROPERTIES PANEL

It is a contextual panel which changes depending on which tool you are using. It is one of the most important toolbars in Dreamweaver. It can be opened and closed from the Window menu

THE DOCUMENT TOOLBAR

Includes code, split, and design/live view. In addition the other icons on the page change depending on which view you are working in. It also shows all RELATED files; cascading stylesheets and JavaScript file, associated with the HTML pager on which you are working. NOTE: In Dreamweaver CC and before you cannot edit your page in LIVE view.

THE DOCUMENT WINDOW

This is where the web page is created. Don't confuse the name of the file with the Title of the page. At the bottom of the document window we see the extremely important Tag Inspector, preset magnifications, preset window sizes, which can be modified in the Preferences. **The Tag Inspector** allows us to select an HTML tag and make sure we are editing this tag when we move to the CSS Designer panel.

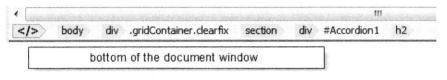

bottom of the document window

PANELS AND PANEL GROUPS

Panels are organized into panel groups and can be reorganized, float, expanded, etc. The two most important panels we work with are the Files panel and the CSS Designer panel.

THE FILES PANEL

The files panel gives you access to all of your documents, both Locally (on your computer or flash drive) and Remotely (on the web host on the Internet). You must always add or delete files from your site while working within Dreamweaver.

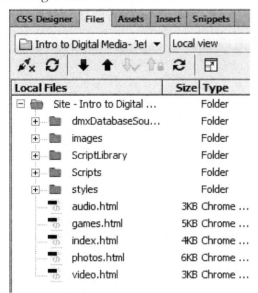

THE PREVIEW IN BROWSER BUTTON

This button allows you to Save, Upload, and View a webpage with a single click. It is part of the tag selector at the bottom of the document window. When you click the globe icon it uploads the current file and launches the default browser to view it.

Note: The Preview in Browser button appears at the top of the document window in Dreamweaver CC 2014.

THE CSS DESIGNER PANEL

The CSS Designer panel contains ALL the styling information about whichever item you currently have selected on your page. For example in the picture below I have selected a paragraph on my index (or home) page. The CSS Designer panel shows the values of certain properties that are affecting the appearance of the paragraph. These include the padding around the paragraph. You can edit ALL the properties applicable to any item on your webpage but you would deselect the Show Set checkbox (currently selected in my example picture).

CLASS FIFTEEN HOMEWORK- 5 POINTS

For the remainder of the semester you will be taking all the work you have done over the course of the semester and placing it on various web pages. You have a total of 100 MB of storage space on the student server. **Make sure your slide-show and resume videos are LESS THAN 95 MB combined.** You must also remember to bring your flash drive

MODIFY AND UPLOAD YOUR SLIDE SHOW/SOUND CLOUD PAGE (1 POINT)

1. Open Dreamweaver and make sure you are working in your defined site. You should see a folder at the top of your Files Panel on the right side of the Dreamweaver interface. Make sure all of the files that you downloaded last week are inside of your Local folder.

2. Open audio.html and complete steps in option one OR two below

OPTION ONE- EMBEDDING YOUR MUSIC STORED ON SOUND CLOUD

   a. Go to the soundcloud.com and sign in.

   b. Choose your Profile under your username and you will see the sound files you have uploaded

   c. Click the share icon under the song you want to place on your web page

   d. Choose Embed from the popup window

   e. Select the code in the text field below, right-click and choose copy

   f. Go back to the audio.html page and choose Code View.

   g. Click and drag your cursor through the ENTIRE iframe tag in line 50 of the Code.

   h. Select Edit> Paste

   i. Go back to Live View. Double-click on the placeholder text at the top of the page and write a paragraph (at least three full sentences) discussing and describing your Sound Cloud composition.

   j. Select File> Save

   k. Click the Preview in browser icon at the top of the page. This should upload your page to the website.

   l. Make sure that your Sound Cloud composition plays and that all links in the navigation bar are working.

m. Close your page and exit Dreamweaver.

OPTION TWO- SLIDE SHOW OPTION

a. Choose the Code View button at the top of the Document window

b. Click and drag your cursor through the ENTIRE iframe tag in line 50 of the Code.

c. Hit the DELETE key

d. With the cursor in line 50 choose Insert> HTML5 Video

e. Look in the Video Properties below the document window and click on the Browse for file icon next to Source and navigate to the location of your mp4 file. Note: It should be labeled hw9.mp4

f. Click on the dropdown next to Preload and change it to auto.

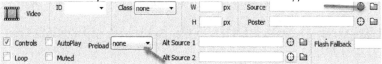

g. Go back to Live View. Double-click on the placeholder text at the top of the page and write a paragraph (at least three full sentences) discussing and describing your Slide Show.

h. Select the Audio tab in the navigation bar at the top of this and ALL other pages and change the name to Slide Show

i. Select File> Save All

j. Select ALL FIVE html pages in the Files panel and click on the up arrow to put the files to the student server.

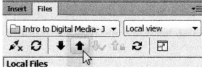

k. Make sure that your Slide Show video plays in the web browser and that all links in the navigation bar are working.

l. Close your page and exit Dreamweaver.

MODIFY AND UPLOAD ALL PAGES WITH LOGO, TITLE AND FOOTER CHANGES, INDEX PAGE WITH PARAGRAPH, AND SELFIE (2 POINTS)

Open Illustrator and convert **class6.ai** file into .PNG files you will use as the logo for your site

1. Open **class6.ai.**

2. Select File> Export> Save As Type> PNG

3. Click on the checkbox **Use Artboards** and the radio button **All**

4. Click Export and save into your images folder of your local site

5. When the Export dialog box appears leave default settings making sure that Background Color is Transparent and click OK.

6. **Close and Quit Illustrator**

Open Dreamweaver and **make sure you are working in your defined site.** You should see a folder at the top of your Files Panel on the right side of the Dreamweaver interface. If you do not you MUST choose Site> Import Site and import your site definition.

1. Make sure all of the files that you downloaded last week are inside of your Local folder.

2. Double-click on **index.html** in the Files panel and place your cursor on the existing logo on the page.

3. In the Properties panel below the document window choose the Browse for Folder icon next to where it currently shows images/logo. png and point to YOUR logo

4. Double-click on the text in the paragraph beneath the heading Introductory Paragraph and write a minimum of one paragraph describing yourself and your interest in Digital Media, and one paragraph on the primary skills you have learned related to Bridge, Photoshop, Illustrator, and Dreamweaver. It should be a minimum of 250 words in total. REMOVE all the filler text on the page including my images.

5. Replace the image placeholder on the right side of the index page with a photo of YOU.

6. Open up your other four pages; games, audio, video, and photos.

7. Follow the steps above and replace the logo with your own

8. Change the text in the footer (bottom of the page) to include your name and the year

9. Change the Title tag.

10. In Dreamweaver CC you change it on the top of the document window

11. InDreamweaver CC 2014 and 2015 you change it in the Properties panel

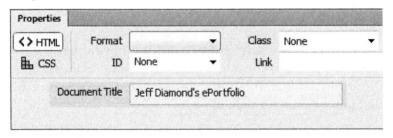

12. Select File> Save All

13. Select ALL FIVE html pages in the Files panel and click on the up arrow to PUT the files to the student server.

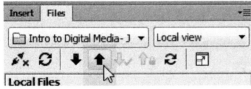

PLACE YOUR FLASH GAME ON THE GAMES PAGE AND UPLOAD TO THE STUDENT SERVER (1 POINT)

1. Select File> Open > games.html

2. Select the gray box in the middle of the page.

   `<body> <div.gridContainer.clearfix> <article#main.fluid> <p> <object#FlashID>`

3. Click on FlashID in the tag selector under the Document window.

4. The Properties panel below should show the settings indicated below.

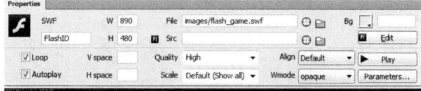

5. Click the Browse for file icon to the right of where it says images/flash_game.swf

6. Navigate to the location of your flash game. It should be called **class10. swf**

7. Click the Preview in Browser icon . It should ask if you want to save the file and upload it to the server. Click OK.

8. Check that the URL in the address bar is student.santarosa. edu/~yourusername/intro_digital_media/games.html

9. Save and close games.html

PLACE YOUR VIDEO ON YOUR VIDEO.HTML PAGE AND UPLOAD TO THE STUDENT SERVER (1 POINT)

1. Open video.html

2. Choose the Code View button at the top of the Document window

3. Click and drag your cursor through the ENTIRE iframe tag in line 50 of the Code.

4. Hit the DELETE key

5. With the cursor in line 50 choose Insert> Media> HTML5 Video

6. Look in the Video Properties below the document window, click on the Browse for file icon next to Source and navigate to the location of your mp4 file. It should be labeled hw10.mp4

7. Click on the dropdown next to Preload and change it to auto.

8. Go back to Live View. Double-click on the placeholder text at the top of the page and write two sentences or more discussing and describing your Video Resume.

9. Click the Preview in Browser icon at the top of the page. It should ask if you want to save the file and upload it to the server. Click OK.

10. Check that the URL in the address bar is **http://student.santarosa. edu/~yourusername/intro_digital_media/video.html**

SEND ME THE LINK TO YOUR PAGE

1. Navigate to the Assignment page

2. Click on the **Submit Assignment** Button at the top of the Assignment page.

3. Copy your **index.html link** into the Website URL text field and click the **Submit Assignment** button.

I check ALL your pages from the index page. The links to all your other pages must work from here.

CLASS SIXTEEN: WEB DESIGN & DYNAMIC IMAGE GALLERIES

STYLING WEB PAGES

Without styling, a web page is nothing more than plain text on a screen organized in a hierarchy. The styling of the website is key to providing the design, look and feel of a site. This is accomplished with Cascading Stylesheets. In this class we will learn to use a combination of color schemes and built-in styles using the CSS Designer in Dreamweaver, to create attractive websites.

USING COLOR SCHEMES TO CONTROL WEBSITE COLOR STYLES

If you are not familiar with the Paletton.com application, try to play with it first. It is designed to create palettes of colors that work well together according to classical color theories. The Paletton Live Colorizer allows you to use the Paletton engine within your own projects. Let your site's users to colorize a template, tables, sheets, web/page design, fliers, any creative graphic design, fabrics, decorations etc. To do that, easily insert the simplified version of the Paletton application to your project, and get the palette data as a JavaScript object suitable for storage or further processing.

CREATING WEB IMAGE GALLERIES

While there are a variety of approaches one can use to create web image galleries, the best ones allow photographers to "set it and forget it". You are going to utilize "back-end" technology that allows you to access your photos that are stored in the cloud and have them displayed on a webpage on your website.

CLASS SIXTEEN HOMEWORK

MODIFY A WEB PORTFOLIO (5 POINTS)

Examine the <u>Web Photo Gallery</u> and create your own gallery following the steps below:

Watch this video demonstration <u>How to Create a Photo Gallery</u>

GO TO THE GOOGLE COLLECTIONS WEBPAGE

1. Click Sign in

2. Either Sign in or click Create account

3. Click Your Collections

4. Click Create A Collection

5. Name the collection **Intro to Digital Media Photo Album**

6. Visible to: Public

7. Click Create

8. Click the Photos icon under Add to this collection...

9. Either upload the files from your computer or choose your Google Photos

10. Click Add button at the bottom of the set of images

11. Click Share

12. Click Name of Album link

13. In the URL bar at the top of the browser window copy the set of numbers after albums/ and paste it into a text file for later

LAUNCH DREAMWEAVER (IF IT IS ALREADY OPEN, CLOSE IT AND RE-LAUNCH IT) AND OPEN PHOTOS.HTML

1. Open **photos.html**

2. Go to line 41 and replace **jdiamond57** with your Google username. Note: Replace the Google username 2 times in this line of code.

3. Replace the string of numbers after **/albumid/** with your copied string from step 13 above. Note: Replace the string 2 times in this line of code. Also there should only be numbers in the string, no letters.

4. Go into Live view and place your name where it currently says Photos by: Jeffrey Diamond

5. Save the page

6. Click the Preview In Browser icon to upload the file to the server

7. Anytime you need to change the content of your Web Gallery, launch a browser, navigate to your Google Photo Album and modify the contents of the album. You do not need to change your photos.html web page

8. Navigate to the Assignment page

9. Click on the **Submit Assignment** Button at the top of the Assignment page.

10. Copy your **index.html link** into the Website URL text field and click the **Submit Assignment** button.

FINALS WEEK: COMPLETING YOUR ELECTRONIC PORTFOLIO

FINAL EXAM AND PROJECTS COMPLETE/ OPPORTUNITY FOR EXTRA CREDIT

1. **Complete** Final Exam (MUST be taken in class. **20 points**)

2. Check your website according to these criteria:

   a. All links from all pages must function

   b. Photo Gallery should function

   c. Flash Game should function

   d. Slide Show or Sound Cloud File should be uploaded and functional

   e. Video Resume should be completed

   f. Color Scheme should be consistent on all pages

   g. Video must include:

      • Opening Title

      • Transitions

      • Your video clip with ultra keying

      • Moving or static background

      • Product Shots

      • Appropriate transitions

      • Lower Third title

      • Background music

      • Closing credits/contact information.

3. Compress your entire website folder

   • Windows- right-click > Send to > Compressed Folder

   • Mac- right-click > Compressed Folder

4. Navigate to the Assignment page

5. Click on the **Submit Assignment** Button at the top of the Assignment page.

6. Click the **Choose File** button and select your **zipped file** then click Open

7. Click the **Submit Assignment** button.

8. Check the grades page. If you are within 5 points of the next letter grade, you can boost your grade by: completing an extra credit assignment (up to 6 points if fully completed correctly).

Congratulations! You have completed a very ambitious program and learned a lot about digital media; what you like, what you don't. Hopefully, this program has helped you understand the world of digital media and helped steer your course for your future in this exciting and dynamic field. Best of luck.

Jeffrey Diamond
Santa Rosa Junior College

CPSIA information can be obtained
at www.ICGtesting.com
Printed in the USA
LVOW13s1504230617
539169LV00010B/991/P